KLAUS BALKENHOL

Britta Schöffmann

KLAUS BALKENHOL

THE MAN AND HIS TRAINING METHODS

Translated by Reina Abelshauser

TRAFALGAR SQUARE
NORTH POMFRET, VERMONT

This English edition first published in the United States of America in 2007 by
Trafalgar Square Books
North Pomfret, Vermont 05053

Printed in China

Originally published in the German language as *Klaus Balkenhol:
Dressurausbildung nach klassischen Grundsätzen* by Franckh-Kosmos
Verlags-GmbH & Co. KG, Stuttgart, Germany, 2007.

Library of Congress Cataloging-in-Publication Data

Schoffmann, Britta.
  [Klaus Balkenhol. English]
  Klaus Balkenhol : the man and his training methods / Britta Schoffmann.
    p. cm.
  Includes index.
  ISBN 978-1-57076-378-6
  1. Dressage horses—Training. 2. Dressage. 3. Balkenhol, Klaus. I. Title.
  SF309.5.S36 2007
  798.2'3092—dc22

                                2007029699

Photo Credits:
Klaus Balkenhol (pp. 9, 12 *bottom*, 14, 16 *bottom*, 17, 19, 23, 24 *bottom*, 26, 27
bottom, 28 *bottom*, 29, 32, 34 *bottom*, 35 *bottom*, 36, 37, 38, 41, 42, 44, 45 *bottom*,
46, 47, 48, 49, 50 *bottom*, 51, 53, 54, 55 *bottom*, 57 *bottom*, 58, 60, 63, 65 *bottom*,
69, 73, 78, 83, 86, 92, 94, 105 *bottom*, 148); Elke Berg (p. 55 *top*); Arnd Bronkhorst
(p. 71 *bottom*); Jan Gyllensten (p. 68); Werner Ernst (pp. 50 *top*, 74, 79 *bottom*, 81,
89, 126); Karl-Heniz Frieler (p. 61); Alois Müller (pp. 7, 10, 11, 15, 16 *top*, 18, 20, 22,
24 *top*, 27 *top*, 28 *top left and right*, 31, 33, 34 *top*, 35 *top*, 39, 40, 43, 45 *top*, 52, 56, 57
top, 62, 65 *top*, 66, 70, 71 *top*, 75, 77 *top*, 79 *top left and right*, 81 *top left and right*,
82, 84, 87, 90, 91 *top left and right*, 93, 96, 98, 99, 101, 102, 103, 104, 105 *top*, 107,
109, 111, 112, 113, 114, 116, 117, 118, 120, 122, 123, 124, 129, 133, 134, 136, 137, 138,
140, 141, 145, 146); Julia Rau (p. 64); Bärbel Schnell (pp. 91 *bottom*, 95); Britta
Schöffman (pp. 76, 77 *bottom*, 85); Julia Wentscher (p. 72); the illustration on p. 12
is from *Reitkunst im Wandel* by Sylvia Loch.

Jacket design: Heather Mansfield

10 9 8 7 6 5 4 3 2 1

MY PHILOSOPHY

TRAINING—
FROM FOAL TO DRESSAGE MOUNT

THE TRAINING SCALE
IN DAILY PRACTICE

MOVING UP TO GRAND PRIX—SYSTEMATICALLY

WHEN RIDING BECOMES ART

RESOURCES

KLAUS BALKENHOL — BEING ONE WITH THE HORSE

The idea to write a book about Klaus Balkenhol was inspired by my longtime friendship with the Balkenhol family. I had long been fascinated by his way of working with horses as well as riders, his brilliance in the saddle, and last but not least his exceptional life—from growing up as a farmer's child, to becoming a "simple police officer," to rising to international fame and earning recognition in the highest ranks of the horse industry and the sport of dressage. It's incredible what can be achieved if one has a dream and never loses sight of that goal.

A simple biography, however, would not have done Klaus Balkenhol justice. It would have been—as much as I respect his fascinating life—too little. I wanted to make his work—the way he deals with horses, his message as a rider and trainer (which I'm lucky enough to experience first hand when occasionally training with him in Rosendahl)—the core of this book.

Today, Klaus Balkenhol stands as one of the few international advocates of classical training principles. He faithfully adheres to the elements of the Training Scale, and convinced of its value, he fights for it, and isn't afraid of making himself unpopular if necessary. In a time when spectacular displays of movement—however achieved—are favored in order to gain high audience ratings, he has remained modest and humble. For him, riding means being one with the horse; it means harmony instead of sharp spurs. Let's hope that in the future the sport of dressage is characterized by this harmony. The horses deserve it.

BRITTA SCHÖFFMANN

HORSES HAVE GREATLY
ENRICHED MY LIFE

When looking back on my childhood, I often think of how I used to walk behind the plow pulled by the farm horses, dreaming of someday being one of the great riders at the top of equestrian sport. Back then, it was only a dream for me. In order to simply get as close as a spectator, I often picked potatoes so I could use the extra money I earned to buy a ticket to a regional horse show.

I think that these types of experiences, in particular, instill value in a thing. They also teach you to sympathize with anyone who attempts to "work his way up" and accomplish a goal through diligent effort. This awareness makes you more mature and tolerant in all your dealings.

Without my riding I probably never would have had the opportunity to meet the politicians, leading businessmen, artists, and millionaires I have had contact with over the years. I have never felt any envy when meeting such people, as I am proud of my past and the experiences I have had in the course of my life. I have also met many very wealthy fellow riders who have never made me feel as if they were superior in any way. In the dressage ring, before the judges, we are all the same— even though I've never been able to afford to buy expensive horses. In the end it's all about "riding correctly." That is all that counts.

The events, places, and people I've been able to experience with horses I would, without a doubt, repeat in my next life (if there is such a thing!) In fact, the only thing I'd do differently is try to understand horses even earlier in my life in order to make fewer mistakes.

Of course, throughout my career there were mistakes that could have been prevented, but on the other hand, these led to gained experience and insight. If I had to look at a timeline today, I'd say that I'm very happy and satisfied with my life.

I've always received great support from my family, especially from my wife, Judith. She has participated in shaping my career as a rider and has been a good critic—not always a comfortable one and sometimes provoking, but always in order to help me better myself. At this point I'd like to thank her in particular.

Judith and Klaus Balkenhol

Also my daughter, Anabel, who with all our showing sometimes did not receive the full attention she deserved, but still has always been patient and supportive.

And, of course, I'd like to thank my greatest teachers: the horses. They've taught me to put aside my own interests, remain humble, and that a life with nature and horses is what constitutes real wealth.

Finally, I'd like to thank Britta Schöffmann, who never tired of trying to snatch a free spot in my busy schedule. Without her persistence this book probably would never have come to fruition.

In the pages that follow I don't reinvent the principles of classical dressage training and the Training Scale—that would be presumptuous. I do, however, try to explain my point of view and compile the experiences that I've been lucky to have with horses over the years.

Klaus Balkenhol

KLAUS BALKENHOL

MY PHILOSOPHY

FOLLOWING CLASSICAL PRINCIPLES

It seems like everybody is talking about classical dressage; about preserving the purity of its principles. But what does the term "classical" actually mean? Does it mean "old" as opposed to "new"? Outmoded as opposed to modern? Or, does it refer to the foundation of horsemanship?

Derived from Latin, the term "classical" generally refers to historical epochs that are accredited with great achievements and perfection. And do not all riders strive to achieve absolute perfection in their actions as riders? "For me this definition definitely hits the core of the matter," says Klaus Balkenhol emphatically. "The sport of riding, regardless of the discipline, can never lead to perfection without adhering to classical principles. And even if one does follow all the classical rules and guidelines, the art of riding is still difficult; the individual traits of each horse will show even the best rider his limitations and revert him to a novice. To this day, I have learned something from every horse I've been allowed to ride and train. And I'm still learning.

"One can only dream of, and strive for reaching true perfection. Few riders are ever really granted this. The rider who says, 'I know how to ride,' has not understood the complexity of this sport, which in its perfection almost becomes an art. I don't think

The high art of classical dressage captured in an oil painting from 1868. It shows Waloddi Fischerström, head rider at the Swedish Court.

Nikolaus Balkenhol at the age of two-and-a-half, still safely in Daddy's arms, together with his brother Heinz and their dog Janko.

HOW IT ALL BEGAN

On a windy, cold winter morning, December 6, 1939, a future Olympic gold medalist uttered his first cry at Ross Manor, in the town of Velen, Münsterland. There had been some delay because the umbilical cord had strangulated the little boy in such a way that he—already turned blue in his face—almost suffocated. It was thanks to the intervention of a stouthearted midwife that the boy survived.

that the span of one human's life is enough to really, fully master this art. It must be enough to simply understand a little more every day, to learn more, to face new challenges and—on the best of days—solve them."

Classical in both form and content: Klaus Balkenhol on the black stallion, Escorial.

Everyone had really been expecting a girl, to be called "Käthe." But since the baby wasn't in any hurry to be born, Josef Balkenhol was pretty sure that his wife, Maria, was going to give birth to a "Nikolaus" instead. And he was right.

THE EARLY YEARS

Together with his three siblings, Heinz, Christa, and Rita, little Nikolaus—nicknamed "Klaus"—grew up at Ross Manor, a generously sized farm (formerly owned by the aristocratic Landsberg-Velen family), where his father worked as an administrator.

Horses were part of the Balkenhol children's daily life. Already at the tender age of five, Klaus could be seen riding the work horses—

CLASSICAL DRESSAGE
VS. COMPETITIVE DRESSAGE

The usual challenges of working with horses have been further complicated by "modern" trends in equestrian sport, which have further and further digressed from the classical principles during the last few years. When business profits and large crowds outweigh the classical principles, the quest for perfection in horsemanship is forgotten—in favor of striving for fame, money, and medals.

Training "classically" means to strengthen the horse in accordance with its natural ability.

So, could one say that the classical art of riding is the antipode to competitive riding? Balkenhol doesn't think so. "Both belong together, even if they recently have been slightly drifting apart," he insists. "The classical training principles are the foundation for all riding. Through them, a horse acquires the necessary strength to perform the movements demanded in high-level competition without injury.

"Training 'classically' means to strengthen the horse in accordance with its natural abilities, thereby creating a solid foundation to build on, regardless of riding discipline. For this reason, I don't consider classical dressage and competitive dressage to oppose each other. Rather, I believe they form a symbiosis.

"This idea, however, must also plant itself in the heads of riders. It's nonsense to say that the competitive side of the sport can do without classical principles. Conversely the same is true because everything classical for its own sake would end up in a museum! This can't

Aerial view of Ross Manor in the 1950s.

Little Klaus Balkenhol in second grade with his teacher, Mühlensiepen, and classmates on the stairs of Velen Castle.

be our goal. The sport is what keeps our passion for equitation and horses alive.

"The only thing we must be sure to do is to preserve the horse's natural grace through the classical training principles. In my opinion, this includes caring for horses appropriately, providing good

Klaus Balkenhol's main concern is to further a horse's natural talents—here on US team mount, Kingston.

powerful draft horses with stoic minds—to the fields, then walking beside the plow, and helping as much as he could. As a child, he was already learning how to deal with horses by observing their nature and their language. "I remember well a horse named Zilli," Balkenhol reminisces. "She liked to bite, but we got along well. Back then she taught me that I had to become a horse's friend if I expected the horse to cooperate."

ANIMALS INSTEAD OF SCHOOL

Klaus Balkenhol's parents actually had a different career in mind for their son. They wanted him to remain in school and be trained in something that had nothing to do with agriculture. But early on, Balkenhol wanted to do "something with animals" and stood his ground. At age fourteen, after completing the compulsory number of years in school, Balkenhol became an agri-

Although in his late 60s, Klaus Balkenhol still rides every day.

training, plenty of love, and knowing and understanding the Training Scale. The Training Scale remains the ultimate measure of quality because only with its help can one manage to develop a horse under saddle carefully and responsibly. This is not something I or some old 'cavaliers' have invented—it's a system that has evolved over centuries and has proven itself over time."

Classical and competitive dressage should go hand in hand. They should stimulate each other. A former mounted policeman, Balkenhol has demonstrated convincingly that this is possible. With a style deeply rooted in classical dressage, and as an ardent admirer of riders and trainers such as Felix Bürkner (1883–1957), Richard Wätjen (1891–1966), Wilhelm Müseler (1887–1952), Otto Lörke (1879–1957), Otto Hartwich (1917–1989), Willi Schultheis (1922–1995), and Egon von Neindorff (1923–2004), he has earned multiple World Championship titles and Olympic gold medals. In addition, his roles as trainer and coach have provided him innumerable successes in the discipline of dressage. As coach of the German dressage team, Balkenhol led them to gold in the Olympics as well as the World Championships. He trained Nadine Capellmann for more than thirteen years and helped mold her into a multiple-time German champion, a European champion, and a two-time world champion. And, with his help the US riders have developed into a powerful team—Balkenhol has led them, too, to the top.

None of these achievements, however, are reason for the passionate rider, trainer, and breeder to "rest on his laurels." The schism between

The young Klaus Balkenhol was always taken with horses—here he is shown with "Schatzi."

cultural apprentice at Ross Manor.

"It was a great time, but also a tough time," he remembers. His salary was 20 German Marks a month (about $14.00 US/£7.00 UK). At that time, it really wasn't possible to make more. Plus, young Balkenhol had other pressures: "My father demanded that I, son of the administrator, became a role model for the other apprentices." This meant being the first one in the barn to milk the cows in the morning and the last one to leave competitive and classical riding ideals, which has been apparent for quite some time, prompted Balkenhol, together with a few like-minded people, to found "Xenophon," an association dedicated to preserving and furthering classical riding culture, in the summer of 2005 (www.xenophon-classical-riding.org). The objectives they formulated are in accordance with Balkenhol's own deep convictions:

We are highly concerned about the fact that work with horses in inter-national competition is often not in accordance with the well-being of the animal. Reports about the use of schooling and training methods that ig-nore significant aspects of animal rights and welfare accumulate in the media. Many judges do not adhere to the valid principles of classical equi-tation, thus failing to obey the rules and regulations of the Fédération Equestre Internationale (FEI), which are in effect throughout the world. These judges prefer the mechanical perfection of a horse ridden in con-trolled tension to the suppleness of the genuinely well-schooled horse.

The dominance of commercial motivation in the sport means that young horses are brought along much too quickly. The horse is being denigrated to an item of merchandise, and riding to a line of business.

Classical equitation does not need to be reinvented. It has been con-ceived and tested in meticulous detail over the course of centuries. It re-mains firmly anchored in the Principles of Riding and Driving of the Ger-man National Equestrian Federation (FN), and also applies at international FEI level. Although there is indeed some scope for individual interpretation, we must stipulate quite clearly that there are no fundamental

the field in the evening. There were no "son privileges." Remembers Balkenhol: "That time in my life taught me discipline."

FIRST RIDING LESSONS

Despite the hard work, young Balkenhol enjoyed his time at Ross Manor. The third and last year of his apprenticeship, however, he completed elsewhere. He moved to the Wenke Farm in Albachten, Münsterland, where he was able to

In the evenings he rode the work horses.

Klaus Balkenhol had a particularly close relationship with Goldstern.

alternatives to classical equitation. Anyone who ignores this ancient wealth of knowledge and experience, and instead tries to achieve dubious aims quickly by means of tricks and technical cunning, is acting irresponsibly—against the health and well-being of the horse, against ethical principles, and against the FEI body of rules.

"really ride" the work horses, which were Warmbloods. For the sixteen-year-old horse enthusiast, this was a great opportunity.

Balkenhol was allowed to go to the State Riding School in Münster, which was directed by Paul Stecken and at that time had the only indoor arena in the region, for lessons. He rode after his long work days and got up early in the mornings to work in the field—now for 60 Marks (about $42.00 US/£21.00 UK) a month. Although he was now

paid more than he had received in the beginning of his apprenticeship, it wasn't enough to live without worries, even back in 1956. "At that time I became aware of the fact that I had to take my life into my own hands, that nobody else would do this for me," says Balkenhol. "When I ran out of money, there was nobody who helped me out. And when I worked sloppily, I didn't get any recognition."

The understanding of the relationship between our horses' health and classical training principles has been lost for the most part. Instead of recognizing that the causes of physical problems can often be traced back to one's own incorrect riding, many riders have the symptoms treated by veterinarians or equine hospitals on a regular basis.

As the knowledge of how to train horses responsibly disappears, so does the aesthetic and spiritual beauty of the art of riding, and the feel for being in harmony with a relaxed horse that's willing to perform.

These developments in equestrian sport are alarming. We will fight against them and ask all lovers of horses who believe in the ethical principles of riding and classical horsemanship to act in kind.

This proclamation is more than just words, which Balkenhol unremittingly demonstrates in the numerous seminars and lectures he gives around the globe, pointing out the deplorable state of affairs and making an effort to encourage every rider and horse-lover to think. "Horses belong in my life, as does the air that I breathe," he explains. "Not only have they determined and influenced the course of my life ever since I was a child, they have also shaped me, and opened a world to me that I probably would never have entered without my riding.

"Over the years, I've become more patient—at least with the horses I work with. I now know that it's not that they have to learn to understand me, but that I must learn to understand them. Although there were times in my youth when I looked for quick success and in-

It's not the horses that have to learn to understand the humans, it's the humans who have to learn to understand the horses.

A MATTER OF LIFE AND DEATH

The riding lessons Balkenhol was taking were so important to him that he refused to admit to anyone he had developed terrible saddle sores after a particularly intensive session on Harras, a work horse that was also a talented jumper. He continued with his training, blood

In his youth Klaus Balkenhol was a daring jumper rider.

Klaus Balkenhol immersed in "shoptalk" with his daughter, Anabel, who he calls "Belli."

from the sores soaking his underwear and breeches. At home, he sought relief by secretly cooling the open wounds with water. Each morning his work day began at six o'clock. In the evening, he continued to ride. Day after day this went on—until he finally broke down, unable to move from the hips downward. An ambulance took Balkenhol to the nearest hospital, where the diagnosis was severe infection and blood poisoning. He remained in the hospital for six weeks, and was then allowed to return home to his parents, on crutches. He suffered a relapse twice and had to return to the hospital. "My life was on the brink," Balkenhol remembers 50 years later.

Balkenhol recovered with the help of a physician from Dülmen— and was soon back on horseback. In the fall, months after his first visit to the hospital, he completed his apprenticeship and passed the required test.

stant progress as a rider, I did eventually learn that everything takes time. The rider cannot give the horse a timetable, rather the horse gives a timetable to the rider.

"I owe it to these wonderful animals to give a little back to them. Training horses according to their natural dispositions is so important because it demonstrates respect for them."

If you visit Balkenhol and his family at home in Rosendahl, Germany, you can rest assured that the horses there enjoy the very best treatment. At the Balkenhols', they're more than just riding horses, partners in sport, breeding products, or elements of someone's profession—they're the emotional, as well as the financial center around which the Balkenhols' entire lives revolve.

From the kitchen window you can see the farm's lush pastures; from the living room and patio you have a direct view of the dressage ring. Every room in the house speaks of horses; all around are bits and pieces of the Balkenhols' all-consuming passion. The latest horse magazines from all over the world are piled up, the walls are laden with horsey photos, and on the shelf next to the big, old fireplace (where often a cozy fire flares), one finds more books on horses and riding than on any other subject.

"We just can't live without them," Balkenhol says, his face beaming. He admits that he not only arranges his rare free time with his wife, Judith, around important equestrian dates, he also usually doesn't go without horses when he's on vacation.

"Klaus Balkenhol is extremely good at tuning into both horse and rider. Unlike some other instructors, he doesn't try to pigeonhole his students, but adjusts individually to every rider and every horse. On top of that, I think he's a really great horseman. The horse's well-being has utmost priority for him. I've learned an awful lot from him."

PRINCESS NATHALIE ZU SAYN-WITTGENSTEIN
Short-listed for the Danish Olympic team, two-time Olympic reserve rider, student of Balkenhol's for seven years

THE DECISION

Balkenhol worked as a farmer for three years. Then his life took a turn. "One day when plowing the field, stumbling along behind the horses with the ropes around my neck, I asked myself if this was really the life I wanted to lead," he says.

The 20-year-old's growing doubts were accompanied by a call to serve in the Federal Defence Force. But "shooting and killing" was not for Balkenhol. He discovered that he could spare himself military duty by committing to the police force for three years. "Also," he admits, "the police force offered an entry-level salary of 265 Marks (about $187.00 US/£92.00 UK), while the army paid only 60 Marks."

His decision was made. Balkenhol took the qualifying test—and passed—and the farmer became a policeman.

DEVELOPING TRUST

For a long time, Klaus Balkenhol—who served as a policeman in the German Civil Service in the greater Düsseldorf area for almost 30 years—didn't have an opportunity to breed horses, or buy foals and raise them. Living in a metropolitan environment, he not only didn't have the time for it, but space was also an issue. "The farmer inside me always wanted to breed my own horses," Balkenhol says.

When he finally purchased and moved to a farm just outside of the Münsterland village, Rosendahl, in 1996, Balkenhol laid the foundation for making his dream come true. These days there are always three to six youngsters—some are bred by him, others are bought or are there to be raised and trained—cavorting in the generous pastures on his farm. "It's always fascinating to be around foals and then follow along as they age and change," he says. "After all, a horse's life is permanently 'stamped' by its youth."

Despite his obvious soft spot for the foals, he attaches great importance to educating them properly. "They must learn to obey from the very beginning," Balkenhol insists. "Apart from the early lessons learned from the mare, the foal's education must be provided by a human being. It's important, however, that this is done without using force and instead through patient teaching. Foals that have had intense contact with humans from the very begin-

TEN MEN SHARING A ROOM

The time he spent at the police academy in Münster opened up a new and completely different life for the young Balkenhol. He shared his room with nine other men. There was no privacy, and there were tiresome drills and rigid working hours,

Klaus Balkenhol (on the far right) had to get used to the youth-hostel-style group accommodation in the police academy.

When Klaus Balkenhol goes through the barn, all the horses stick out their heads, wanting to say "hello."

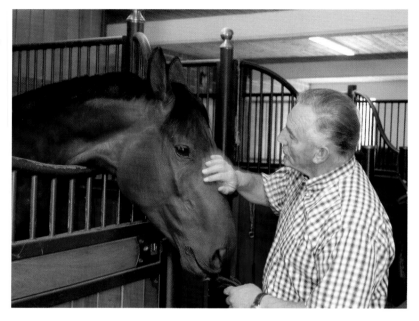

ning, that have been well guided by them and so have developed trust in them, are generally easily introduced to the rider when it is time for work under saddle."

In order to create a sense of familiarity and subsequently build trust in his horses, Balkenhol enters each stall daily, including the foals' stalls. Patting each horse briefly, offering a treat and checking if

When a member of the riot police in Bochum, Klaus Balkenhol was responsible for the Borgward trucks.

but also camaraderie, fun, and many new impressions. "It was a good time; it formed me," he remembers almost 50 years later. "There I learned that one has to subordinate oneself, yet stick to one's personal goals."

A year later the farmer's son moved to the large city of Essen, Germany. There, in the middle of the Ruhr district, he initially underwent additional training in technical engineering and transportation before transferring to the riot police everything is all right are part of the horseman's daily routine. The only exception to this rule is when Balkenhol is traveling (on horse-related trips, of course!)

The youngsters on Balkenhol's farm learn from an early age that their handler is their boss as well as their friend. "In order to ensure this respect from the very beginning, our foals learn to be haltered, led, and tied as soon as possible," explains Balkenhol. "We generally first tie the foal while the mare is eating her grain. If the foal is tied while standing beside his mother, he usually remains relatively still and relaxed, and grows accustomed to his freedom being restricted in a playful way and without pressure."

STARTING YOUNG HORSES STRESS-FREE

Klaus Balkenhol also feels it is tremendously important to do things "playfully" when first introducing a young horse to a rider. He rejects force and the stress related to it completely. "For this reason," he says, "I don't have a fixed date in mind when determining the 'when' of a horse's training. I introduce the horse to a rider when the horse is mentally and physically ready—and this can be different from horse to horse. Horses do not physically mature before they're seven or eight years old. Mares often develop differently than stallions; big horses differently than small ones. One often forgets this fact. It's a

in Bochum, Germany, where as a driver he was responsible for three trucks.

The farm, the horses, and the riding were things of the past. "I didn't even think about them anymore," he admits.

SOMETHING IS MISSING...

In Bochum, Balkenhol never thought about his riding. The service, his colleagues, his police truck, the new sense of "power" in uniform—all this was fulfilling enough for the 23-year-old. But when it came time for newly-trained policemen to be assigned to different stations, Balkenhol asked to go to Coesfeld, closer to his parents—and closer to the horses again. But his wish was declined. It wasn't matter of experience to know—when watching the horse moving freely in his pasture—if he's ready to be introduced to a rider, or if he needs more time to develop. After all, we wouldn't make a very young, underdeveloped child work.

"Sadly, this issue often takes a backseat these days, and trainers try to follow a rigid pattern when breaking young horses. When this happens, it's not the horse that takes precedence, but the money to be won or earned."

At Balkenhol's farm, young stock are allowed all the time they need. Most often they're started the late summer/early fall before they turn four years old. To begin, they are longed, initially in a snaffle bridle and a surcingle; later with a saddle. Since Balkenhol does a lot of groundwork prior to the introduction to serious training (leading, tying up, longing in a halter, loading and traveling on a trailer), it usually goes smoothly. "Once in a while a young horse is not yet ready to deal with the rider's weight and shows this by being extremely irregular in the rhythm, refusing to go forward, or throwing his head," Balkenhol says. "In such cases, you should be patient, turn the horse back out in a field, and postpone your training plans for a few weeks or months. When you start again, such problems might have disappeared on their own—simply because the horse has had more time to mature."

As a matter of principle, the "time factor" plays a vital role in Balkenhol's work with horses. "Regardless of a person's level of training, he must never place undue pressure on himself or his horse.

I introduce a horse to the rider when the horse is mentally and physically ready, not necessarily when he has reached a certain age.

standard to serve near one's hometown, as the authorities feared cronyism.

So, in 1963 Balkenhol ended up in the Mettmann municipal police, in Hilden. He wasn't quite able to abandon his roots, and so looked for a room to rent on a farm in the neighboring town of Langenfeld. "I lived with the Schorks," he says, "a very nice family, for little money,

Klaus Balkenhol tried to be transferred to his hometown (shown with his family, second from the right).

Things take as long as they take. Sometimes it's shorter, and sometimes longer. Even when working with a talented young horse that seems capable of anything, a person must be careful and proceed with caution. Even the most talented youngsters are still 'children.' They lack the real strength necessary to truly perform what they may be predisposed to offer."

The "boss" always keeps an eye on his assistants, making sure they ride the young horses in a manner that's appropriate for their age and don't overtax them.

including meals. At the end of my own workday, I helped them with the farm work." Balkenhol was happy with the scenario. Until 1967 he remained a patrolman in Hilden, never giving a second thought to the mounted police squadrons. "I thought they were all stupid and only did weird kinds of stuff," he admits now with a grin. He did, however, meet a man who was looking for somebody to ride his horses. So Balkenhol ends up in his barn—and there had a fateful encounter.

JUDITH

She was only fifteen years old. She was gangly, skinny, and crazy about horses. Judith Pfeiffer's father worked at the Ministry of the Interior, her mother was a housewife, and neither of them suspected that Judith was to become Mrs. Klaus Balkenhol one day.

Judith and Klaus Balkenhol met in a riding arena. "When I tried to give her a few tips, she just rode straight over me, totally unnerved,"

Judith Balkenhol was already an ardent rider when she was a teenager.

The first time a rider mounts a young horse should be done extremely calmly. Usually the horse is positioned in a corner with his head toward the wall. While Balkenhol holds and praises the horse, the rider quietly mounts. Then Balkenhol holds the horse until the rider is sitting in the saddle, when he then leads the horse forward for a few steps at the walk.

Judith and Klaus Balkenhol were married August 30, 1968.

Balkenhol says with a laugh. "Later on, we would get along fantastically since we both loved horses—but in the beginning there wasn't more than casual friendship."

This changed rapidly, however, and the friendship turned into love. Five years later, on August 30, 1968, they were married. Judith was only 20 years old, and her new husband 29.

Balkenhol feels the best example of this is a horse with a natural talent for collection. The rider who confuses a horse's physical predisposition for collected work with fully developed carrying power and asks the horse to collect too early in his training will end up having a big problem. This might manifest itself in resistance, reluctance, laziness, unrideability, or illness.

Before a horse is able to correctly collect, he must first be systematically strengthened through gymnastic exercises based on the Training Scale. Anything else will lead to a dead end sooner or later. For this reason it is a trainer's most noble duty to recognize when a horse is able to—mentally and physically—work at a higher level.

A horse must be capable of completing a task mentally as well as physically.

AVOIDING OVERTAXING THE HORSE

In order to avoid overworking the young horse and yet slowly strength and condition him, Klaus Balkenhol uses a three-phase system. To begin (Phase One), the horse is generally familiarized with humans and various groundwork, which gradually intensifies (including longeing in a halter) until the horse is approaching two years old.

Phase Two consists of introducing the horse to the bit, saddle, and the rider's weight, and the first six months of training to follow. The

THE MOUNTED POLICE SQUADRON

It was Judith Balkenhol who brought up the topic of the "mounted police squadron," even before the two were married. Her love of horses was addictive. The couple spent many free weekends at Germany's big shows—Aachen, Wiesbaden, Hamburg—standing by the warm-up arenas, marveling at the great riders. There the idea of the mounted police squadron took on a more concrete form, and in 1967, Balkenhol applied for the training squadron in Cologne—and got the job.

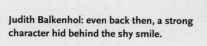
Judith Balkenhol: even back then, a strong character hid behind the shy smile.

horse is only lightly ridden during the week after the first mounting (only for a few rounds of the arena, at first led by an assistant, then later without a ground person). As soon as the process of tacking-up and riding is accepted and considered "ordinary" by the horse, ridden sessions are reduced to two to three times a week. When not ridden, the horse is longed, free jumped, and of course given ample turnout in a pasture or paddock.

Phase Three begins, depending on the horse's level of maturity and development, approximately six months after the first time he is

AUXILIARY REINS AND YOUNG HORSES

"I don't believe in using auxiliary reins on young horses. A young horse needs his neck to balance—some horses more than others. Some horses drop their neck after their first or second riding session, while others require days or weeks. If the rider relies on auxiliary reins at this point, he only hinders the horse's balance. Further, the tension this creates aggravates the balance problem instead of resolving it. One must reject draw reins or side reins categorically when starting a youngster. If a horse is prone to throwing his head, a rider may temporarily use a martingale. If the problem continues to exist, the rider must look for the cause. If the head-throwing horse has no health problems, it might be that it's simply too early for this horse to be started under saddle. In such cases the horse simply must be given more time to develop."

KLAUS BALKENHOL

IN COLOGNE—STILL A LONG WAY FROM CLASSICAL PRINCIPLES

In Cologne, one of the riding instructors was an ex-hairdresser named Grimm. "You must pull in the front of the horse; this will make his head come down," was one of his tips. The police squadron approach was quite "un-classical."

In addition, everything was organized and run by rigid rules. Rookie officers were only allowed to ride the old horses, and Balkenhol was assigned a horse named Ikarus that had a cardiac defect and was dreaded by other officers because of his tendency to buck his riders off. Balkenhol noticed that Ikarus' saddle pinched him and coaxed the harness master into giving him another one—and overnight, Ikarus turned into a saint.

Balkenhol's supervisors noticed that the young man from Münsterland seemed to know something about horses. From that point for-

Riding forward-and-downward is part of the gymnasticizing groundwork at Balkenhol's facility, and is not only used for young horses (Anabel Balkenhol on a five-year-old mare, left) but also for trained Grand Prix horses (US rider Steffen Peters on Floriano, right).

mounted (generally after the horse has turned four years old). From this time on youngsters are increasingly worked under saddle, until they are ridden for 30 to 45 minutes daily. In addition—after all, by now it's spring again—they're ridden outside the arena and turned out regularly.

"Although this way of starting young horses might take a little longer than is customory in some other facilities, I've only had good experiences with it," claims Balkenhol. "As a basic principle, I'm against giving the horse a 'crash course,' because one always runs the risk of wearing the horse out. Of course, there are many three-year-olds these days that look as if they were twice as old—and they are

ward, he was allowed to ride "retraining projects," including Ferdi, a horse that had "an appointment with the butcher" since he constantly reared and acted up. Balkenhol recognized that poor Ferdi suffered from severe dental hooks. At that time, however, it was commonly thought that a horse must chew them down by himself and didn't require a veterinarian or dentist. On the spur of the moment, Balkenhol grabbed a hoof rasp and took things into his own hands.

How lucky for Ferdi, because he almost instantly became rideable, and "I'm sure this prolonged his life for a few years," says Balkenhol.

ON A DETOUR TO DÜSSELDORF

By the end of his time as a trainee in Cologne, the word had spread that Balkenhol was quite a good rider. He was transferred to the mounted police squadron in Wuppertal and was supposed to help the riders

It's important to recognize a horse's signals before a mistake is made.

worked as if they were. Most of these horses, however, will down the road vanish into thin air."

To make sure that this does not happen to his horses, and those of his students, Balkenhol pays careful attention to each animal, virtually "listening" to them. "Even if training is heading the wrong direction," he says, "initially, horses will just keep on going. One must recognize and interpret their signals in time, and react accordingly."

For Balkenhol, such signals are:

- ▶ **Unusual resistance**
- ▶ **Sudden, alleged "stubbornness"**
- ▶ **Nervousness**
- ▶ **Tension**
- ▶ **Grinding of the teeth**
- ▶ **Tail swishing**
- ▶ **Ears constantly back**

"Every time a horse behaves differently from how he normally does, it could be a sign of physical and mental overload. A horse just responds in his own, natural way," says Balkenhol. "If, for example, a young horse suddenly and consistently evades upward with his head—provided that the saddle and bridle fit well and his teeth are in good shape—his back muscles are overstressed. The rider who begins to fight with this horse and keeps working him

> "I'm fascinated by Klaus Balkenhol's ability to tune into each and every horse. He's always perfectly calm and can certainly teach something to every horse and further it."
>
> **CAROLA KOPPELMANN**
> Long-listed for the German Olympic team, professional rider

there improve a bit. Balkenhol, however, didn't feel quite comfortable there. There was no indoor arena and real "training" wasn't possible. Plus, on patrol rides he found that all the horses were amazingly willing to stop at convenience stores and bars—it appeared the squadron there was a bit too "fun-loving" for Balkenhol's taste. At this point, he wanted to work more seriously, and approach riding more seriously. "I wanted to leave," he says, "and I asked to be transferred to the mounted police squadron in Düsseldorf."

His wish came true at the end of the 1960s, partly through the help of his father-in-law. Although his father-in-law's influence got him accepted into the Düsseldorf squadron, it didn't make the transition any easier. The other officers welcomed Balkenhol with

Police squadron leader, Otto Hartwich.

according to the motto, 'I have to ride him through this!' runs the risk of building up too much lactic acid in the muscles (one of the most common problems in young horse training, by the way). Instead of using force, the rider should take a break or even go back to a less challenging training step the horse may have already mastered.

Instead of using force to achieve a movement, it is better to take a break or go back a whole step.

"In the long run this leads to the end goal more quickly. If a young horse shows common signs of discontent—grinding his teeth, swishing his tail, or laying his ears back—the rider must find the cause in order to ever succeed and reach a state of harmony with the horse. This does not mean the rider should sacrifice consistency, or even

According to Balkenhol, relaxation breaks "on the buckle" are important for the horse's mind and body. (Nathalie zu Sayn-Wittgenstein on Digby.)

skepticism. The "top dogs," especially those who were considered to be experienced riders, let the newcomer with connections (who was said to be a good rider, to boot) feel their rejection.

Balkenhol found help and support in the leader of the mounted police squadron, Otto Hartwich (see photo, left), who became a fatherly friend to Balkenhol. "From him I learned a great many things about riding and about horses," says Balkenhol. "He has greatly influenced me. A former instructor at the Cavalry School of Hanover, he followed the Classical Principles of riding down to the smallest details. He was strict with the horses but never unjust or mean. He had endless patience and was able to make every horse dance, without a lot of effort. He taught me that each movement must be preceded by work on the basics. Hartwich knew about the complexities of training horses and knew how to put them together like an orchestra at a con-

Digby a little later in a working phase: here shown in a relaxed extension...

strictness when training a horse. However, he must always react appropriately and never disregard the fact that a horse—all training and goals set aside—is always simply a horse, and so also reacts as such. That's his nature."

Regardless how much training and ambition a rider might have, he must always remember first and foremost to allow a horse to be a horse.

Klaus Balkenhol knows what he's talking about. In his active career as a rider, trainer, and coach he has often had to deal with horses that haven't always made it easy—in spite of their obvious talent and genius. Goldstern, Balkenhol's famous Olympic police mount, was a "pistol," and Gracioso, who later accompanied Nadine Capellmann to international success, was not an easy horse, either. Farbenfroh, who

cert. He wasn't a competitive rider—he was an artist."

DEBUT WITH HEIDI

Otto Hartwich knew that the young rider wanted more than to just be a patrolman on horseback. At this point in his life, Balkenhol rode at the level of regional Second Level tests, but was eager to learn more,

Police officer Balkenhol, at the age of 25, shown with "Heidi" ...

...and here in highest collection. The intensity and emphasis of the work are determined by the horse's character, among other things.

eventually became a two-time world champion, was known to have his own strong opinions.

To recognize, accept, and adjust to each and every horse's individual characteristics is an art and requires a great deal of maturity. "Every horse has its own rhythm," says Balkenhol. "I could write an entire book about each of them."

The horse's individual rhythm also determines the "tempo of training," i.e. the timetable that determines the rate of increased demand on the horse. "It depends on how strong the individual horse has become as work has progressed," Balkenhol explains. "There are

I could write an entire book about each horse I've ridden in the course of my life.

so Hartwich allowed him to ride his own patrol horse, Donaumädel, a Hanoverian mare by Goldfisch. "'Heidi,' as we called her, was a great horse with beautiful movements," Balkenhol remembers. For him, the newcomer in Düsseldorf, it was a great honor to ride this horse in particular. He was allowed to show Heidi at Second Level in five shows a year within the police precinct of Düsseldorf.

...and later achieving his first success at Second Level.

horses that mature quite early, and find the tasks under saddle easier. Other horses need more time, perhaps because they grow at a more sporadic rate, suddenly becoming extremely big, or maybe they remain mentally a little behind their physical capabilities.

"For this reason," he goes on, "I don't have a recipe with detailed ingredients for training horses. I simply try to never lose site of the Training Scale as it is applied to an individual horse. I use the same rule in my coaching, as it applies to the individual rider, as well.

"A rider should be very advanced if he plans to train a young horse. Sadly, it's become more and more common these days for inexperienced riders to purchase a young horse with the goal of training and riding it themselves. It's only logical that this will not likely lead to success. After all, a young horse and an inexperienced rider don't have a common language. Both have to learn this language, which is only possible if they learn from a partner who is perfectly fluent already. The less skilled I am as a rider, the more I have to learn from the horse. The more skilled I am as a rider, the more am I able to teach the horse. I continue to recommend to all riders to only purchase a horse whose level of training appropriately matches their own ability—for the horse's sake. And in addition, riders should always be open to accepting help from another, perhaps more knowledgeable and experienced individual as they progress."

Dressage training means working a horse according to his natural predisposition and willingness to perform.

Klaus Balkenhol (on the inside) riding Heidi with his former colleague Josef Offermann riding Tosca in a Pas-de-Deux.

CHOOSING THE RIGHT (DRESSAGE) HORSE

The fact that basic dressage training is a great way to prepare any horse for his future "career," regardless of discipline, is nothing new, and to Klaus Balkenhol, is not debatable. "Every horse should receive some solid dressage training," he says, "as it increases rideability on the one hand, and promotes health on the other. Training a horse in

The first police mount to make a career as a dressage horse: Rabauke ridden by Klaus Balkenhol in 1977, was already a "modern-type" dressage horse.

LISTENING TO THE HORSE

Heidi was followed by Liebeslust (known as "Tosca"), a very complex grey mare by Jason xx. She showed young Balkenhol just how difficult and frustrating riding could be. When he rode her in a snaffle bridle, she hardly lowered her head, but when Hartwich rode her, she was supple in the poll before he even mounted her, and all her movements seem playful and effortless.

Balkenhol was dissatisfied and unable to figure out what he was doing wrong. "I want to be able to do what you are doing," Balkenhol said to his mentor.

His teacher told him to listen to the horse in order to be able to give the right aids at the right time. "If you are able to do that," he promised his pupil, "then you've understood part of the horse's language."

dressage doesn't mean that the horse has to be trained to Grand Prix level, but rather that he should be worked according to his athletic predispositions and general willingness to perform. If a particular horse is found not to be suitable to pursue 'higher education,' he should not be forced against the odds. After all, not every child who knows how to play the Flea Waltz on the piano will turn out a 'Mozart.'"

Many an ugly duckling can turn into a magnificent swan when trained well.

The question is how do you know if the Flea Waltz is the pinnacle of a horse's accomplishments, or if he is meant to attain higher goals? This is a question Balkenhol has dealt with time and time again. "To evaluate three- or four-year-olds, or even younger horses, and predict whether they have the potential to become international Grand Prix champions is incredibly difficult, if not impossible," he says. "Whoever claims to know that a particular three-year-old horse is destined for stardom is lying. There are certainly horses that early on seem to be equipped with all the right qualities, but they often fail at some point in the course of their training, even when ridden by the best trainers, because the majority of horses have a problem or limit somewhere. There are also an innumerable number of talented horses that completely vanish from the scene due to improper training, while others, who might have been rather unremarkable in the beginning, turn from ugly ducklings into magnificent swans when trained properly."

The Olympic mount Granat, ridden by Christine Stückelberger, was such a horse, as well as Gigolo (under Isabell Werth), and Rabauke (under Balkenhol himself). Although they may not have

PROFESSOR TOSCA

Balkenhol learned the horse's language step-by-step, word by word. Tosca became one of his best teachers. She punished every mistake her rider made and was less forgiving than Oleander, another police mount that Balkenhol was allowed to ride at that time. Although Olean-

In the 1970s, Klaus Balkenhol proved that police mounts could also jump, here shown on the gelding Oberon.

Klaus Balkenhol riding Little Big Man, a horse with a great mind and a lot of talent who sadly passed away much too early.

been aesthetically beautiful or anatomically perfect, they were all endowed with outstanding basic gaits and—what often counts more—exceptional character.

der was quite a stiff fellow, he learned all the movements and responded better to the rider's aids than Tosca. So Balkenhol took what he learned from Oleander and transferred it to Tosca.

Another lesson came from Sultan, a fellow officer's grey gelding that was difficult to ride through the poll and round. The search for the "why" discovered that the horse suffered from chronic pain in his abdominal muscles—the consequences of a previous colic surgery—and therefore didn't relax his back. Balkenhol worked him thoroughly and managed to decrease the stress on Sultan's muscles by making him step more under his center of gravity. "Suddenly I knew that I was on the right track," says Balkenhol. "As I gained the ability to ride Sultan and Tosca, my ability to ride others horses grew as well."

The ambitious young man also successfully jumped obstacles during this time, usually on the impressive gelding, Oberon.

The chemistry between rider and horse—here Balkenhol on US horse, Kingston—must be right.

LOVE AT FIRST SIGHT

For the next three years Balkenhol was with the mounted police squadron in Düsseldorf, showing occasionally at First and Second Level, and once in a while jumping 3' courses. The rest of his time was filled with riding lessons, patrol rides, and mounted deployment at soccer games, demonstrations, and the German Carnival.

Balkenhol was 31 years old when the squadron chief, Otto Hartwich, took him to the police riding school's department in Cologne where young horses, bought as two-year-olds, were introduced to the basics of mounted police work for one year before they were sent off to the different squadrons. There, Balkenhol was allowed to select a horse. He chose a chestnut gelding that looked quite unremarkable and was just being shod by the farrier. "From the first moment I saw him, I thought he was beautiful, and he had a trusting nature,"

"What's most important to me besides good, rhythmically pure, uphill basic gaits and a natural willingness to collect," says Balkenhol, "is a horse's character and personality. A horse must have a nice eye, and be sensitive, stouthearted, and good-natured. He should like 'his' humans, because then he'll be willing to perform for them."

It is clear to any observer that Balkenhol's horses like "their" human very much. Whenever he enters the barn, a sudden wave of movement goes through the rows of stalls. Ears are pricked, a sense of calm spreads, and every horse waits trustfully for his turn to be close to his master. "I enjoy those moments," says Balkenhol. "Especially at night when I do one last round by myself to check on everything before I go to bed. The invisible communication, this kind of deep listening—it really has something magical to it."

The moments of invisible communication between me and the horses are magical to me.

Of course it's not enough that a horse and rider like each other. They also must suit each other. "In order to achieve something with a horse, suitability is very important," Balkenhol emphasizes. "Horse and rider should benefit from each other—an inexperienced rider should take advantage of the experience of a well-trained horse. And an inexperienced horse learns better, and more likely with long-lasting success, if it is ridden by an experienced rider. In the equestrian world, experience is irreplaceable. If horse and rider are suitable matches, then the only thing left that they need is the right chemistry."

A well-known example of the importance of chemistry is the gelding, Beauvalais, formerly owned by German Olympian Heike Kem-

Balkenhol remembers.

That gelding, named Rabauke, was also a good mover, but Balkenhol would only realize that later. In the fall of 1971, at three-and-a-half years old, Rabauke moved to the Düsseldorf facility. It was the beginning of an exceptional career.

Rabauke and Klaus Balkenhol became a well-established team.

mer. Although a top rider, she wasn't the best match for the horse, and she sold him. In a roundabout way he eventually ended up in Spanish rider Beatrice Ferrer-Salat's hands. She tried him and immediately thought, "This is my horse." Her feeling was right on: the pair moved up to the top tier of international dressage, crowning their partnership with an individual Olympic bronze medal.

One should love horses in order to do them justice in every phase of their life.

However, regardless of the horse's talent and rider's ability, their chemistry, and ambition (being "hooked" on the sport)—all this will only lead to true success if there is respect for the horse on top of everything else. "One should love horses in order to do them justice in every phase of their lives," insists Balkenhol. "A rider must never put his ambition above the horse's needs. He must know a great deal about horses in general, about their characteristics as social beings and, especially if one competes, about their physical well-being. Only he who understands how the horse's anatomy, physiology, psychology, and training interrelate is able to responsibly school a horse to his potential. For me, following the Training Scale is crucial in this. It is the only method that has been systematized through the centuries and is based on the horse's anatomy, guaranteeing that the horse is trained gently and, above all, naturally."

THE TRAINING SCALE

- ► Rhythm
- ► Looseness/Suppleness
- ► Contact
- ► Impulsion
- ► Straightness
- ► Collection
- ► Letting the aids through/"Coming through"

Balkenhol (on the left) used his patrol rides in the woods as additional time for his dressage training.

HALF-PASSES IN THE WOODS

Riding Rabauke, Balkenhol was finally able to transfer everything he learned from the other horses he'd ridden. He trained diligently, both in his riding lessons in the morning as well as during patrol rides in the Grafenberger Forest. The others smirked, saying he "rode like Spilles"—a colleague who practiced movements anywhere and everywhere—but his effort paid off. Rabauke and Balkenhol's first show

THE TRAINING SCALE
IN DAILY PRACTICE

GRACIOSO AND RHYTHM

Most alleged training "innovations" aren't really new but were actually already dismissed as useless centuries ago.

In the course of his career as a rider and trainer, Klaus Balkenhol has produced a vast array of horses that have achieved national and international success. Every one of them was trained according to the basic classical principles of the Training Scale. Balkenhol has always rejected industry trends—not because he's old-fashioned, but because he's seen many things come and go in his equestrian life: people, methods, and even downright oddities. "Sometimes I look around and I am amazed," he explains during one chat next to the fireplace. "People try so many 'new' things with horses, forgetting that essentially, horses haven't changed over the past decades. And, these alleged innovations often aren't so new after all! Most of them were tried years, or even centuries ago and dismissed then as useless."

Like other great masters before him, Balkenhol remains staunchly loyal to time-proven methods. "The Training Scale, with its requirements for rhythm, suppleness, contact, impulsion, straightness, and collection, provides the path that turns an untrained foal into a good riding horse," Balkenhol emphasizes. "Not only is the Training Scale a valid guideline for the training of young horses, it is in fact the framework of dressage. No matter how advanced a rider is, no matter how young or old or how well or badly trained a horse is—this frame-

In 1972 the family is complete: daughter, Anabel, called "Belli," is born.

together—the regional championships in the Renish town, Eggerscheid— ended with a first place. "At that time, it was my biggest success ever," Balkenhol says, smiling.

This isn't quite true. In 1972 he celebrated another victory (an even greater one) together with his wife: the birth of daughter, Anabel. As the true horse enthusiasts they were, the new parents took "the poor child" to shows from day one. ("Which certainly didn't hurt me!" Anabel says today, laughing.)

work must be built carefully and worked over again and again. If necessary, one must go back to the basics in order to be successful in the end, even if this means returning to 'square one'—rhythm."

When discussing "rhythm," Balkenhol likes to mention Gracioso, a horse that eventually became successful under Nadine Capellmann. The chestnut gelding had already passed through many hands when Balkenhol purchased him in 1993 as an eight-

If necessary, one has to go back to the basics in order to succeed in the end.

Basic gaits with a secure rhythm, as shown here at the walk, make it easier for a horse to start a dressage career.

A beaming Klaus Balkenhol after a victory at Fourth Level in Heiligenhaus, his second victory of the day on Rabauke.

SUCCESS IN MÜNSTER

The first victory with Rabauke was followed by others, first at Third Level, then at Fourth Level. In 1976, the equestrian regional newsletter, "Rheinlands Reiter Pferde" published an article about the "riding policeman."

year-old. "He was difficult," he says. "He had a pounding trot with little ground coverage, a tendency to lose the rhythm, and problems going forward. He also had a bad canter that tended to be four-beat, especially to the right, and a 'runny' kind of motion in general. Only his walk was good—regardless how tense he was in the other gaits, as soon as you transitioned to walk, he performed a calm and rhythmically pure walk."

Balkenhol remembers exactly why he purchased the difficult horse: "I saw a horse that had an enormous amount of energy and showed great moments in collected movements, perhaps 'paddling around' a little bit here and there, but then immediately showing a super walk. This made me purchase him."

In Gracioso I saw a horse with a great amount of energy and great moments in collection.

Gracioso didn't disappoint the man who discovered him. Under Balkenhol he won numerous Grand Prix tests, and with Nadine Capellmann (who would eventually purchase him) he won innumerable tests at Grand Prix level, as well as national and international titles and medals. However, it took a very, very long time to get there. "When he first came to us, Gracioso was an introverted horse and didn't trust people," Balkenhol says. "He stood in his stall with his rump toward the door. He was very reserved—he seemed to have 'had enough' of humans. One always had the impression he had retreated into a shell. It was as if he had found a platform on which he could arrange himself and the things he needed to get by, and he had no desire to step off this platform."

Balkenhol entered the Westphalian Club Championships, which caused some of his older colleagues to react with skepticism. They believed that this show would bring him back down to earth. But, in front of a thrilled audience—who had never before seen a policeman in uniform in such a competition—Balkenhol won the Prix St. Georges and the Intermediaire I.

Klaus Balkenhol doesn't dedicate his entire self to equestrian sport—his heart also belongs to his daughter, Anabel. (Here, a rare shot showing both of them riding one horse, although the overall expression is still a bit stiff and "wooden"...)

But Balkenhol wanted more from this horse. He wanted to pull him out of his isolation since he suspected he was capable of great things. Balkenhol's years of experience told him that rhythm under the rider—and the suppleness that follows—could not be achieved without first gaining the horse's trust in humans. So he spent a lot of time on his newly purchased horse. Gracioso wasn't only worked carefully, he was also taken by the hand (rather, by the hoof). "I tried

In the beginning, Gracioso didn't trust people.

At the beginning of his training with Balkenhol, Gracioso had problems with rhythm.

THE INVESTIGATION

By now, the media were falling all over themselves, avidly reporting about the successful "riding police-man." However, it seemed not everyone was thrilled with Balken-hol's triumphs. The day Balkenhol was to load Rabauke on the trailer and set off for the big German Championships in Münster, the chestnut was lame. Although he was wearing egg-bar shoes, a long nail was imbedded deep in one of the horse's hind frogs. The veteri-narian felt it was not a coincidence, and suggested the possibility of sabotage. The police investigated, but in vain. "For the first time," says Balkenhol, "I realized what envy can do."

THE TELEPHONE CALL

Second, Third, Fourth Level and above—Klaus Balkenhol learned everything by himself, figured out many new movements by himself,

In order to encourage Gracioso to trust different riders, he was also ridden by Judith Balkenhol—here he is shown stretching down in a relaxed manner.

to be near him as often as possible," Balkenhol remembers. "I visited him in his stall, petting and touching him everywhere, until I got the feeling that he was beginning to like it. I was trying to get to know his nature; this was a way of building trust between us."

After about a month of these "stall visits," Gracioso started to turn around when Balkenhol entered his stall, and he would sniff him interestedly. Slowly, very slowly his sullen and standoffish attitude was crumbling away.

and acquired a lot of knowledge from books and successfully translated it to the saddle. His horse, Rabauke, now also performed piaffe, passage, and all the tempi changes.

However, "the man from Münsterland," the policeman in uniform, the "Nobody" in the realm of dressage, wanted to achieve more. He called the German Olympic Committee for Riding (DOKR) in Warendorf and asked if he could participate in a clinic given by the German team coach, Willi Schultheis.

The Ministry of Interior gave Balkenhol the green light. For the first time in his life, together with Rabauke, he drove to Warendorf, the center of equestrian sports in Germany, walked around the "holy facility" stiff as a poker and impressed by everything. "I was completely awestruck and carefully greeted everyone I came across because I thought they were all great, international riders," he says, smiling.

In his memory, everything is as if it had been yesterday: "Willi Schultheis

The whole Balkenhol family took an intense interest in this shy horse. Judith and Anabel (Balkenhol's wife and daughter) both rode him. "This way," Balkenhol explains, "with time, Gracioso no longer took it badly when different people rode him; he learned to concentrate on and accept each rider.

"However," Balkenhol continues, "he still had problems with rhythm. But because his state of mind was becoming increasingly relaxed, contact had improved, which meant that one could better ride him 'toward' the bit. The cycle of rider's hand-to-poll-to-neck-to-back-to-hind leg was interrupted less and less often, which ultimately is the prerequisite for having a clear rhythm."

Gradually Gracioso gained the inner and outer strength that he needed for dressage.

In addition to the stall "trust building" and daily dressage work (including many transitions, turns, and lateral movements), Gracioso was also longed a lot and ridden outside the arena. This not only helped him develop confidence and balance, it also increased his physical fitness. It was only at this point that he gained the mental and physical strength required to perform the movements demanded in an upper level horse. "Although he was already eight years old when he came to us, he lacked the strength necessary to perform as was expected of him. I think that he had felt overwhelmed by everything that was asked of him," speculates Balkenhol.

Balkenhol's confidence in Gracioso paid off, far beyond his expectations. He eventually successfully competed Gracioso at international Grand Prix level, before his student, Nadine Capellmann, took him

was standing in the corner of the indoor arena, chatting with two professionals. 'Oh, you're the mounted policeman from Düsseldorf,' he snarled. Still immensely impressed, I was only able to utter a feeble 'Yes.' 'Why don't you bring out your police mount,' Schultheis ordered. I rode; Schultheis was silent. Then he got on Rabauke, rode one-tempi changes, piaffe, and passage. When dismounting, he said—and I will never forget this as it made me incredibly proud— only one word: 'Compliments.'"

German team coach Willi Schultheis held Balkenhol in high regard.

When Gracioso had gained enough strength he shined, with expressive collection in particular.

SUDDENLY FAMOUS

Even the television cameras discovered the "riding policeman" and his police horse.

Willi Schultheis was incredibly impressed by the young policeman, and he told the equestrian journalist, Dieter Ludwig—who was in Warendorf at the time looking for news in the sport—that this police officer from Düsseldorf was one of Germany's eight best riders. Ludwig, at that time employed by the Sports Information Service (SID), instantly reported this news about the man in the green uniform, and in 1977, the regional over. With Gracioso, Capellmann won two team gold medals—one European Championship and one World Championship—as well as the German Championship. And Gracioso never ever had problems with rhythm again.

Gracioso's success story shows that rhythm problems can be overcome, provided the rider recognizes their causes and has the knowledge necessary to solve them. "This doesn't mean riders can fix every kind of problem," Balkenhol emphasizes. "One has to be cautious about believing success can be had where others have failed. The best way to determine whether a horse can overcome a problem caused by poor riding or training is to evaluate whether his movement is essentially 'correct' and then not make any compromises in regard to his rhythm or suppleness."

For the rider, coach, and trainer, "correct" movement means: when at liberty in a field, a horse should have perfect rhythm and demonstrate elasticity, loftiness, and ample ground–cover in the gaits (as opposed to short-strided, tense, flat movement with the horse is on the forehand).

One doesn't always do better where others have failed to achieve.

▸ The Walk should exhibit a clear four-beat rhythm, be ground-covering, big-striding, and active.

▸ The two-beat trot should demonstrate impulsion generated by the hindquarters, even in the first trot step. The trot should be forward-and-upward, moving out of the shoulder and covering a lot of ground. The horse's hooves should land in the spots they point to during the "swing phase" of the gait.

The newspapers were filled with stories about the "riding policeman."

An optimal canter covers a lot of ground, as the stallion His Highness demonstrates here.

equine newsletter "Rheinlands Reiter Pferde" published the story, "A Policeman's Self-Promotion" and other daily newspapers featured the article, "Master Rider from the Mounted Police Squadron." Suddenly, gone were the days when Balkenhol was an anonymous rider. He became a flagship for the police force—a poster child. And along with him, the police mount, Rabauke. Balkenhol gave radio and TV interviews. Everybody wanted to report on the "new man in the sport of dressage."

Schulteis wrote a letter to the Ministry of the Interior, managing to get a permit for the talented mounted police officer to enter international shows. Until this point, due to the official regulations of the mounted police squadron, Balkenhol had only been allowed to enter five shows a year within Germany. With Schulteis' aid, Balkenhol received a special permit and financial help from the German National Equestrian Federation.

▸ The canter should be lofty and cover a lot of ground, and the hind legs should angle well under the horse. When working in the canter, the rider should always be sure he has a solid three-beat rhythm, and ride it energetically forward-and-upward.

"'Scraping,' 'dragging,' hurrying, and flat expressionless gaits are not suitable for a dressage horse, and often simply create further rhythm problems when a rider tries to change or improve the gait's motion sequence," Balkenhol says. "Problems at the walk are difficult, but not impossible to fix. It depends on the cause. For example, some young horses initially lose their balance under a rider—which can alter the walk—but find it again after time spent under saddle (as long as the rider influences the horse correctly). Other horses have inherent and deeply rooted rhythm problems at the walk, which you can never get rid of completely.

The individual components of the Training Scale must always be seen together as a single entity.

"The trot, on the other hand, can always be improved to some degree—the rhythm, the ground-cover, and the expression—if the horse is strengthened accordingly. Among other things, the different exercises and schooling movements that you use in training the horse over the course of time can condition the horse appropriately (which movements these are depends on the horse's level of training; they are directly related to the individual components of the Training Scale)."

EMBARRASSMENT IN DORTMUND

Schultheis pushed the talented pair to ride their first Grand Prix at the German Championships in Dortmund. The preparatory clinic, however, seemed to be too much for the chestnut, and the immense

Whereas in Münster everything went well, the show in Dortmund turned into a disaster.

GOLDSTERN AND SUPPLENESS

One of the components of the Training Scale is suppleness or "loose-ness" (Losgelassenheit in German), i.e. the mental and physical relaxation of the horse. This is the foundation and prerequisite for harmonious collaboration between horse and rider. "Over the years I've often had to deal with horses that weren't exactly born with this quality," Klaus Balkenhol admits. Gracioso was one, his famous Olympic mount Goldstern was another, and Nadine Capellmann's star, Farbenfroh, as well. In these horses, there was a fine line between genius and neurotic.

"What would set each horse off was very different, however," explains Balkenhol. "Gracioso had quite a history when he came to us, and was tense simply because he was rather skeptical and reserved toward everybody and everything. Goldstern was different. He was both attentive to his surroundings and dominant: he was very interested in his environment, and sometimes wanted to take over the reins simply to get a better view of what was around and decide himself if he should get excited about it or not. He had an enormous amount of power that had to be brought under control. Farbenfroh was similar in this, although he was extremely sensitive and, in certain situations, rather timid."

Regardless what causes tension in a horse, when it comes to solving

stress resulting from people's expectations made his rider nervous. Though they placed in the Intermediaire II test, the Grand Prix in front of the big audience turned into a complete flop. In the second half of the test, Rabauke pulled his tongue over the bit and happily waved it around. Balkenhol's dreams of a successful Grand Prix debut were shattered. Frustrated, he drove back home, coping not only with the disappointment over the show, but also the sardonic remarks in the newspapers. In some he was termed the "aggressive newcomer," while in others he read: "Placing eighteenth, the anxiously awaited new pair Rabauke and his police officer Balkenhol achieved a succès d'estime. The handsome chestnut was skillfully presented by an almost aggressive, yet not always elastic rider."

A born horseman engaged in a relaxed dialogue in the pasture.

With Linda Tellington-Jones and
Nadine Capellmann on Farbenfroh
at a Tellington Method
demonstration in Reken, Germany.

Balkenhol realized that fame always has two sides—recognition and envy—and the pair didn't compete at Grand Prix level for a whole year. "I just thought we weren't ready," Balkenhol says. It wasn't until the end of 1978, at a show in Iserlohn, when Balkenhol made another attempt at Grand Prix—this time with success. At first go, Balkenhol and Rabauke won second place, behind only Harry Boldt and his Olympian mount, Woyceck.

TOO "UNKNOWN"

Balkenhol's success at Iserlohn was only the beginning. In 1979, Balkenhol became German reserve champion, among other titles, and in the same year Rabauke became the most successful dressage horse in the world. It seemed a textbook

A highlight in the career of the chief police officer: second place at the German Championships in 1979—behind Dr. Uwe Schulten-Baumer jun. and beating Dr. Reiner Klimke.

or preventing it, Balkenhol is an advocate of using only gentle, horse-friendly methods. And, he doesn't hesitate to seek out advice from others—in order to better understand Gracioso's, Goldstern's, and Farbenfroh's neuroses, he turned to world-renowned horse trainer and animal behaviorist Linda Tellington-Jones, whose unique form of bodywork and training is reputed to override common resistances and strengthen the horse-human bond. "It was quite astonishing to see how much the horses changed," he remembers, laughing at the memory of an episode with Goldstern.

ALTERNATIVE METHODS

"Although for me the Training Scale is the one and only main framework according to which the horse should be worked, that doesn't mean that one cannot include inspiration from other alternative areas of study once in a while. I think that anything that brings relaxation and joy to a horse can be used in a manner that supports the Training Scale—but only as long as it doesn't go against a horse's nature and natural disposition."

KLAUS BALKENHOL

career, but the next disappointment was already on the way.

In the days before the European Championships, Klaus Balkenhol and Rabauke were in third place. However, no one nominated them in the pre-selection process. The dressage committee attempted to explain the situation as follows: "Balkenhol doesn't have experience at the international level yet, and regardless of how terrible this sounds, in the discipline of dressage, the judges are—just like in ice-skating or gymnastics—often predisposed and biased. For an unknown rider like Balkenhol, it's impossible to score high."

Despite this road block, Balkenhol and Rabauke finally officially became part of the group of riders from which the German Olympic team was to be selected.

"When Linda worked with Goldstern, he was suddenly transformed, standing there with his ears and neck drooping, totally relaxed. The next day, he was still so relaxed, he didn't go well at all—because now he was lacking the necessary body tension to perform. I said to Linda, 'I guess this didn't work out! Do you think you could change the dose so he's relaxed but doesn't fall asleep?'

"The result was incredible. During the next session she worked with 'Goldi' in a slightly different way, and the following day he was just sensational."

These photos illustrate the difference between a horse reacting with tension when his rider puts too much pressure on him, and the same horse reacting in a supple, willing manner. Photo on left: Tip Top under US rider, Leslie Morse, is unwilling and incorrect in the piaffe (too tight, supporting himself with his front legs, hind legs trail out behind). Photo on right: Tip Top in an exemplary piaffe with the rider applying refined and light aids.

In 1979 Rabauke was the most successful dressage horse in the world.

Even though in busy horse training facilities there often isn't time to really employ such alternative methods in addition to regular work, Balkenhol was inspired by Goldstern's response and to this day continues to include the Tellington Method, and other body- and groundwork in his training. "With Farbenfroh, for example, we worked a lot on helping him get over his ground shyness," he says. "We had him step over plastic sheets, and other strange objects or surfaces. And I'm sure I've dragged the centerline thousands of times at home because he shied from—or jumped over!—the dragged centerlines in competition arenas."

Inconsiderate use of auxiliary reins can quickly lead to a vicious cycle.

When introducing horses to new things, Balkenhol believes you should be consistent in your approach, which should not include force so as to encourage the horse to trust you. "If a horse doesn't trust his rider," he explains, "he'll tense up in unfamiliar situations— this is his way of preparing to flee should the need arise. The rider who reacts to this by applying force causes even more tension in the horse, often to the point of resistance. These are the scenarios that, sadly, then lead to riders resorting to all kinds of auxiliary reins— more force—and horse and rider enter a vicious cycle, which in most cases, they won't be able to escape."

This is why Balkenhol lives by the motto, *trust instead of force*. The mounted police squadron, where he served for over 30 years training all kinds of different horses to become reliable patrol mounts, uses this principle as well. After all, police mounts have to keep their

Another great success: second place at the German Dressage Derby in Hamburg, behind George Theodorescu.

GREAT SUCCESSES

One year later, Balkenhol had become an internationally-known rider and had celebrated great successes, including a second place finish at the German Dressage Derby in Hamburg. Among his fellow riders in the police squadron, he now found recognition and respect, the old "squealers" had retired and the "new" officers appreciated his success and skill as a rider.

RECOGNIZING LOOSENESS/SUPPLENESS

It's fairly easy to recognize if a horse is loose/supple or not:

▸ "Ear play": the ears should move back and forth instead of being directed rigidly forward or flat backward.

▸ Tail: the tail should swing like a pendulum in a relaxed manner, in rhythm with the movement, instead of being clamped, raised too high, or constantly swishing.

▸ Mouth: the mouth should be closed and chomp contentedly instead of rigidly pressed together, chomping in a frenzied manner, or even wide open.

▸ Eyes: the eyes should have a relaxed, trusting quality to them instead of being wide open in fear.

▸ How the horse feels: a horse that's loose (and "moving over his back") allows his rider to sit comfortably.

nerves in situations where "normal" horses would probably completely lose their minds! Riding through fire or straight through raucous crowds are only two of the many challenges they must face calmly and composedly. "It's impossible to make your horse go through flames by beating him up," Balkenhol says. "If your horse is not on your side and doesn't trust you completely, he will never 'conquer' such dangers—he'll flee from them."

The experience Balkenhol gained during his time served as a mounted policeman would strongly influence his future dealings with horses. To this day he never allows young, recently started horses to be

In 1980 a big goal was in sight. The Olympics! Due to political disputes, however, the Olympic Games in Moscow were boycotted by most countries. But Balkenhol kept climbing up the ladder of success, and in the meantime, through his continuous accomplishments, established himself in the sport of the rich and elegant. He was no longer an outsider on the international show circuit but a competitor to be taken seriously—one who put himself in the rankings no matter where he was.

A TRAGIC MISSTEP

Then, in 1982, it was all over. At the international show at Balve, Rabauke slipped during the test and went lame immediately. The diagnosis was shattering: massive knee ligament injury. Rabauke underwent surgery and a long period of rehabilitation from which he recovered, but not enough for another dressage career. The small chestnut with the big heart would never enter a competition again, ridden in the indoor or outdoor arena without another horse present. He always makes sure that an experienced four-legged partner is present. "One must take advantage of the horses' herd instinct," he says. "The cavalry knew this—there, young horses were always only ridden in groups until they had developed trust in their rider and surroundings. And during my time as a police officer we always had a quiet, experienced mount accompany a newcomer.

A horse should only have positive experiences.

"The rider who tries, especially in early schooling sessions, to force a horse to go obediently through let's say a spooky corner, risks affecting the horse in a way that's quite contrary to what he actually wishes to achieve. The horse will now associate this corner with force and fear, and will refuse to go there with even more conviction. It's simply a fact that horses link everything to their memories. For this reason, every experience should be positive. If they aren't, the horse loses trust in people and gradually exhibits more and more tension, which in the end can even take a toll on the horse's health."

The horses that Balkenhol rode over the years all reached an advanced age (the exception being those that suffered from acute illnesses, such as colic). Goldstern enjoyed six years of retirement, and Rabauke was still romping through the farm's fields when he was almost 30 years old—despite the years of training he had received as a police mount in addition to his intensive use as a sport horse. Balkenhol says, "Riding according to the classical principles based on the Training Scale was, and still is, the very best health insurance for horses."

but he remained a good patrol horse for some time.

In 1984, Rabauke was sixteen years old, and the Interior Minister of North Rhine-Westphalia transferred ownership to his rider. Rabauke enjoyed his retirement at the Balkenhol's as one of the family until his death in 1998. The world's first international police horse/dressage mount was 30 years old.

Rabauke with "his" pony, Muskatnuss, enjoying his retirement.

CONTACT—LIGHT LIKE FARBENFROH, HEAVY LIKE RHODOMO

"I could write an entire book on the topic of contact," insists Klaus Balkenhol. If you listen to him in his various roles of trainer, rider, and coach, you can do little else but agree with this statement. In his daily lessons, as well as the many lectures he gives in the US, Germany, and all over the world, it is evident that the third element of the Training Scale is of particular concern to him. Contact is not to be regarded as an isolated element of the Scale, but rather it is embedded in the remaining components. And yet, it remains a huge area of stumblings and jumblings, mistakes and mysteries.

Sooner or later every rider will face problems with contact.

"All riders, regardless of their level of riding, are eventually confronted with 'contact,' and all the problems connected with it," says Balkenhol. "As a matter of fact, a contact that's not been correctly established from the hindquarters is not a real contact at all. To be able to sense this is part of the art that riding can become." Balkenhol regrets that today it seems many riders are content with being capable of simple craftsmanship instead of striving for this art. "Of course, part of the reason might be that it often takes longer for riders to travel the correct path," he muses. "However, the rider who follows this path consistently and patiently will be rewarded in the end. Even if the reward 'only' consists of an indescribable, beautiful, and satisfying feeling of lightness—almost weightlessness—in one's riding, and the resulting harmonious cooperation between horse and rider."

YEARS OF TRAVEL

With the permit to show in more than five competitions a year, Balkenhol was also allowed to train and show horses on the side. The only condition was he must wear his uniform at all shows. After all, the "riding policeman" had turned into a poster child, and neither the

At shows—here riding Ehrengold, co-owned by Dr. Hanno Leimbach— Balkenhol always wore his police uniform.

SEARCHING FOR CAUSES

If a rider suddenly runs into problems with contact, he must look for the cause:
- ► Is the horse's saddle well-fit, adjusted, and not causing discomfort?
- ► Is the bridle adjusted correctly? (For example, a bridle that is adjusted too tightly or that's too small creates painful pressure on the horse's sensitive poll.)
- ► Does the bit fit the horse and is it positioned correctly?
- ► Is everything okay with the horse's teeth?

If the rider has ruled all of these out, the problem is probably caused by his riding!

Klaus Balkenhol categorically rejects the use of draw reins since they result in tight mouths and tense backs, and do nothing but pull the horse together with force.

Chief of Police nor the Interior Minister wanted to miss out on an opportunity.

Balkenhol first accommodated his private clients at the stud farm Eschenbruch in Mühlheim, and later moved into the neighboring barn, which was operated by the Nowak family. "There were people who supported me generously, such as our friend, Hanno Leimbach, who made a horse available to me and helped us acquire a truck," says Balkenhol.

For a time, Balkenhol was quiet on the international front. Nationally, however, he brought many horses successfully to Grand Prix: Mon Petit, Escorial, Aponti, Rhodomo—with all of them, the "riding policeman" from Düsseldorf continued to capture the hearts of the audience.

After one particular clinic, Nicole Uphoff, with her horse Rembrandt, stayed with Balkenhol and trained with him for two years.

At Balkenhol's facility you will not find any draw reins, the "favorite tool" of many riders who look for shortcuts in the training process. He is convinced that, "The rider who uses draw reins in an attempt to 'create contact' is lying to himself. With them one creates nothing but artificial contact, and the horse only 'appears' to be supple at the poll." And there are other negative effects: tight mouths, tight necks, tense backs, and "defensive" strength instead of elegance. "Once such problems have been created through incorrect riding," he goes on, "it's very hard to eliminate them."

Balkenhol knows what he is talking about. Over the years he has had many horses with such issues. One he remembers particularly well is Rhodomo, a big dark bay that was already eight years old when he arrived at Balkenhol's farm. Prior to coming to Balkenhol, the Westphalian gelding had been ridden with the use of a lot of strength and therefore was difficult to get supple in the poll. This gave his new rider—who likes to ride with a simple snaffle bit and light aids—a lot of headaches (as well as back pain!)

"Rhodomo was difficult when it came to contact. He was so heavy and strong that it truly wasn't an enjoyable experience to ride him," explains Balkenhol. So he approached the horse's early retraining in an unorthodox way: instead of riding him in a snaffle, or a snaffle with auxiliary reins, he often schooled Rhodomo in a double bridle. "This was the only way to re-sensitize him to the rider's aids so that I was able to work with him instead of fight with him."

The rider who is patient will be rewarded with a harmonious partnership between horse and rider.

ANOTHER CHESTNUT

In the meantime Balkenhol moved his "civilian" horses closer to Hilden, where he lived. He had a stall wing at Manor Landfrieden for a while before he finally found a temporary equestrian home in a newly built facility in Hilden.

His barrel is still a bit pronounced but his topline is correctly developed: Goldstern as a four-year-old.

Gradually, Balkenhol managed to "convert" Rhodomo, giving him an idea of what correct contact was and creating the necessary physical prerequisites to maintain correct contact comfortably. "The double bridle made him respect my hand a little more," Balkenhol remembers. "Only the double bridle enabled me to get through to him at all with my full halts and half-halts, which are necessary for any sort of reasonable work to be done."

With time Rhodomo began to understand that it's much more comfortable to respond to the rider's aids rather than resist them.

Unsteady in the beginning, Farbenfroh's contact gradually became continuously even.

Balkenhol and the horses remained there, in their own stall wing, for seven years.

There, Rabauke enjoyed his retirement. He was accompanied by show horses such as Ehrengold, the newly acquired Gracioso, Sylvester, Nikolaus, Laudatio, Farbenfroh, and on occasion, a chestnut named Goldstern.

THE GOLDEN HORSE: "GOLDIE"

Klaus Balkenhol had been riding the chestnut, Goldstern (breeder: Willi Altemeier, Delbrück) since 1982. He and his boss, Werner Vatter, had seen the two-and-a-half-year-old Westphalian a year earlier when visiting the young horses at the police riding school in Cologne. They liked the small chestnut with slightly short front legs instantly, and together with the gelding,

This helped transform schooling sessions from combative sport into healthy gymnastic work. "His muscles gradually developed correctly," says Balkenhol, "which in turn benefited his degree of suppleness and thereby also his willingness to cooperate with his rider. Had I opted to use the strength of auxiliary reins as had been done before, Rhodomo would likely have reacted with even more stubbornness and resistance."

Contact is brought about by the rider's entire seat, that is, the interplay of hands, back, and legs.

Balkenhol's ideas worked, and for years he and Rhodomo successfully competed up to Grand Prix level—in a double bridle, of course. At home, however, Rhodomo could eventually be comfortably ridden in a simple snaffle bridle without any problems, just like the rest of his barnmates.

It is not only "heavy" horses that can cause their riders problems. Those that are overly "light" cannot be successfully trained by just anybody. For example, Farbenfroh was equipped with ingenious movement, an incredible amount of expression, nerves that weren't always easy to handle, and in the beginning, an unsteady, insecure contact. "Sometimes he would get strong in the bridle, then very light again, almost too light," his trainer says. It was very important to figure out this problem, since only constantly even contact makes peak performances, such as those Farbenfroh later performed under his rider Nadine Capellmann, possible at all.

"Consolidating correct contact always takes some time," says Balkenhol. "With Farbenfroh, we worked on creating an optimal reac-

Gauner, Goldstern moved as a three-year-old to Düsseldorf, where he was ridden by Balkenhol. Both Gauner and Goldstern were of better-than-average talent, but it soon became apparent that "Goldie" had more capability. However, he was a bit nervy, and he either won his first dressage tests, or they turned into tense disasters peppered with faults.

The little chestnut had the power of a big horse. Balkenhol believed in the Weinberg son.

Whoever was on the road in the Düsseldorf area might well have seen a policeman practicing dressage movements on a future Olympic horse.

Klaus Balkenhol sits supply "in" the horse, framing him with his seat.

Besides daily patrolling, which included duty at parades and soccer games, he built Goldie up systematically as a dressage horse. His movement, his elasticity, and his talent for high collection were exceptional. Gradually they progressed from Second Level to Third Level, and finally Fourth Level and above.

In 1989, Goldstern was ten years old, and he won his first Grand Prix test. A year later he carried his rider to the title of reserve champion at the German Championships. In professional dressage circles, ears were pricked: Klaus Balkenhol was back in the big time. And in 1991 in Münster, he became German champion for the first time.

tion to the giving and taking of the rider's hand. To explain: when the rider 'takes' on the reins, the horse must come back to him; when he 'yields' the reins, the horse must stretch. By riding Farbenfroh forward, combined with lots of transitions up and down, he learned to accept these aids while remaining calm. This gradually gave him the physical strength and maturity to carry himself and his rider in every situation—and always with a light and steady contact." Establishing this contact was absolutely necessary for the horse's future life with Nadine Capellmann—not only because a well ridden horse is characterized by correct contact (or at least should be characterized by it!), but also because Capellmann weighed merely 110 pounds and would not have been able to (though nor would she have wanted to) train a horse on the basis of strength.

A good, correct and effective seat is an indispensable prerequisite to achieving contact. "Contact doesn't only refer to the reins, bit, and the rider's hands, but also to the rider as a whole," Balkenhol insists. "A rider must give the horse contact through his entire seat. This means that his legs must lay gently against the horse's body, his seat must be balanced and supple, and his arms and hands must follow the horse's movement quietly and evenly. This creates a smooth cycle of movement as the horse takes the rider with him. Only this then creates contact."

Balkenhol fully approves of the well-known saying, "Old riders young horses; young riders old horses." He explains why: "Contact

Contact doesn't only refer to the hands, reins, and bit, but to the whole rider.

A DREAM COMES TRUE

Eventually, Balkenhol and Goldstern couldn't be caught anymore. Goldie's name became commonly known, and the policeman, who was once considered a rather exotic figure when he appeared with Rabauke, became an important figure in the world's dressage arenas. After his breakthrough at the German Championships, more great achievements followed, one after another, including the reserve champion in the Freestyle at the European Championships in Donaueschingen and a team gold medal. Once more Balkenhol was considered a potential rider for the Olympic team—and in 1992, he effectively became part of the group chosen for Barcelona.

Shortly before the Olympics, Balkenhol became German champion for the second time, then set off for Spain along with Nicole Uphoff, Monica Theodorescu, and Isabell Werth. The Olympics were a triumph for Balkenhol and his

"Klaus Balkenhol is a real horseman. He is a master in looking at a horse and knowing what to do in order to optimize the horse's potential. In his training he always closely follows the Training Scale, regardless of how advanced a horse is. Furthermore, as a coach, Klaus has a very positive attitude toward horse and rider, which makes training with him very pleasant."

GEORGE WILLIAMS
US dressage team, vice president of the USDF (United States Dressage Federation)

is something that's so immensely important, yet at the same time difficult because it can only be taught to a horse by an experienced rider with an excellent seat. If the rider still has problems with his own seat, he cannot provide the support the horse needs as he learns about contact. And, the younger and less experienced a horse is, the faster contact problems will develop, which can later turn into serious difficulties that disturb the delicate harmony between rider and horse."

Early in his riding career, Balkenhol experienced such a "disturbance" firsthand. At the time, his wife Judith had a horse named Querkopf ("awkward fellow" in English) that fully lived up to his name. "He just wouldn't flex at the poll," Balkenhol remembers. "And the more I tried to make him do it, the more resistant he got. I am now aware that at that time I probably didn't have the experience, security, and skill to help a horse like him. At that time I was simply a young rider on a young horse. It just didn't work out.

"If I had Querkopf now, I would approach many things differently. And I'm sure that with the knowledge I have today I'd be able to figure him out. No horse resists for no reason. Every rider should remember this before pointing an accusatory finger at his horse."

At the Olympic Games in Barcelona Klaus Balkenhol had some of the greatest moments in his career as a competitive rider.

ON OLEANDER, WHO HAD NO IMPULSION

Klaus Balkenhol considers impulsion to consist of the horse's natural desire to move forward, which develops from active hindquarters and continues over a "swinging" back. Generally speaking he believes that every horse has a natural ability for impulsion—one horse may just have more, and another less. However, Balkenhol admits there are occasionally horses that actually have no impulsion at all.

Oleander, an honest, sweet, lop-eared police horse Balkenhol rode during his time in Düsseldorf, was one of them. "He simply didn't have the conformation that would allow him to have impulsion," Balkenhol reminisces, smiling. "Oleander had a steep, restricted shoulder and the general way he was built just didn't enable him to move forward. He had no elasticity, regardless which gait he was in." This, however, didn't keep Balkenhol from gymnasticizing the stiff horse on a daily basis—and successfully! Although the chestnut never competed, he eventually was able to perform quite an acceptable piaffe and passage, and learned one-tempi changes—though his canter always remained awkward and lacking impulsion. "The only thing he never was able to do was a half-pass," says Balkenhol. "Whenever we tried, he somehow always tripped over his own legs."

Oleander was the only horse in Balkenhol's career that had no impulsion and also resisted all attempts to develop it in the course of his

Impulsion manifests itself in natural and relaxed dynamics swinging through the horse's back.

mount, Goldstern: they won a team gold medal as well as an individual bronze. It was a dream come true. When Balkenhol reminisces about Barcelona today, his eyes glow: "That was the greatest experience ever! When I was standing on the rostrum holding my individual medal, I could hardly believe it was

On the same steps where Klaus Balkenhol once posed for a photo of his school class (see p. 14), he was honored upon his return from Barcelona: the stairs of Velen Castle, almost 50 years later.

Relaxed loosening up ...

training. Most of the horses Balkenhol dealt with in the past were like those he deals with today: they all have correct basic gaits and impulsion. The simple reason for this is that these horses either are currently, or are meant to become competitive dressage mounts.

Balkenhol emphasizes that impulsion has nothing to do with the spectacular, exalted "toe-flicking" created for show effect that impresses many people today. Instead, impulsion should manifest itself

happening." Not only were his medals exceptional, but also the fact that he was the oldest participant at the Olympic Games. And, of course, Goldstern was the only police horse present—originally purchased for just under 7000 German Marks ($5,000.00 US/£2,500.00 UK)! "This certainly was and still is unusual for the equestrian events at the Olympic Games," believes Balkenhol, holding a screw he found in Barcelona and kept as a talisman.

BAMBI AND THE GERMAN CHANCELLOR

The public was thrilled by Balkenhol's performance. In 1992 he was not only given the venerable TV and media award, known as the "Bambi," but the Federal President Richard von Weizsäcker also presented him with the "Silberne Lorbeerblatt" (the "silver laurel leaf"), the highest German award for sports achievement. A little after that, Balkenhol was officially welcomed by Chancellor Helmut Kohl.

... develops into expressive impulsion (US rider Steffen Peters riding Floriano).

in correct, natural, and relaxed dynamics swinging through the horse's body from back to front. "Debbie McDonald's Brentina is a nice example of a horse who has kept her natural impulsion even at the highest levels," he says. "She is always light in the hand and on the rider's leg. She doesn't move spectacularly, but she is 'loose' throughout her body, and in her naturalness is as beautiful as Mona Lisa."

ENCHANTING CASTANETS

Balkenhol's hit series as a rider continued. The "riding policeman" from Düsseldorf and his mount, Goldstern, became a trademark, and their Freestyle ridden to music featuring the sound of castanets enchanted both audience and judges. In 1993 the pair won the German Championships and were part of the team that won the European Championships, and a year

Goldstern at his best.

Full of elegance, "throughness," and suppleness: Brentina (ridden by Debbie McDonald) is trained strictly according to the principles of the Training Scale.

later, together with Nicole Uphoff, Isabell Werth, and Karin Rehbein, the World Championships in Den Haag. In the individual Freestyle scoring, Balkenhol earned the silver medal—unjustly so as most of the audience and also some judges saw him winning the show. "Goldie should have won," Balkenhol still thinks in retrospect. But in the Freestyle, nobody could touch Anky van Grunsven, who was carried by the enthusiasm of her fellow countrymen as she performed in her home country.

Balkenhol's life had changed. Now, apart from his police service, the horses were the center of his entire family. Training, education, instruction, and competing made up a large part of his daily life. Wife, Judith, and daughter, Anabel, were willing participants and were always present in the arena.

"Throughout all the years, Judith has been my most honest critic and has also made sure that I kept my feet on the ground," Balkenhol says.

Balkenhol believes it's an art to be able to recognize the different shapes of impulsion, accept them as they are, and then make them more beautiful in a natural way. "Each horse comes with a slightly different form of impulsion," he emphasizes. "One horse might develop his impulsion more from his knee action, while another horse might move more with a straighter front leg. What's essential is the activity from the hind legs, the 'impulse' that sends the horse forward during movement and in the end constitutes his degree of forward desire." The weaker this impulse is, the more the rider has to work on motivating his horse over and over again, while the more energetically the horse steps forward, the more inherent "go" it will have. In itself, this "go" is an advantage. "However," warns Balkenhol. "When horses naturally have *too much* forward desire, many riders tend to 'ride away' this natural impulsion because they are constantly on the brakes." On the other hand, a horse with little impulsion and little "go" generally loses all expression if the rider is constantly "pushing" him.

In her naturalness, Brentina is as beautiful as Mona Lisa.

Too much, too little—there's hardly a horse that was born perfect. So what can the rider do in order to preserve or develop impulsion? "First of all, he must be able to play the Training Scale forward and backward," Balkenhol again emphatically insists. "It's the clavier on which all riding happens. Within this framework it is extremely important to keep the horse responding sensitively to all the aids. Only then can one preserve or improve impulsion."

Always ready for a joke: (left) at a carnival as a "colonel of honor" and (above) in a quadrille at the Robinson Club Fuerteventura after the Olympic Games (on far right of both photos).

"Sensitive" is a key word in Balkenhol's training system. Anyone who observes the master at his work will see what he means by it. Whether applying leg, weight, or rein aids, or a tap with the whip— all must be applied clearly and sensitively. If it is necessary to repeat them, these aids may promptly be given more energetically. For instance, if the horse doesn't respond instantly and willingly to the quiet and gentle forward-driving leg aid, it should be followed by a more demonstrative and energetic leg aid or a tap with the whip.

A horse always must understand what the rider expects from him.

However, the rider must then immediately praise the horse as soon as he moves forward. "It's important that a horse understands what he's supposed to do," explains Balkenhol. "He must understand how to react to a certain aid. He won't learn to understand the aid if he is punished or pestered incessantly. Instead, tell him briefly and very clearly what to do, and then—when the horse reacts in the correct way—praise him immediately. This way the horse remains (or becomes) sensitive, and you will establish a means of communicating with him other than force."

Depending on the type of horse one works with, Balkenhol recommends employing slightly differing approaches. A horse that's overly eager and tends to run out from under the rider must first learn to accept half-halts—he must respond to the rein aid instead of running away from it. Only through half-halts can one control the horse's basic impulsion and desire to go forward. Movements recommended in this case are: leg yielding, shoulder-in, and extensive work at the canter.

In the course of his career, Klaus Balkenhol—here riding Laudatio—produced about 20 Grand Prix horses.

When he was at the height of his career as a competitive rider, the policeman proved his value in terms of teaching and training. One of his most famous students was Nadine Capellmann, the younger sister of Gina Capellmann, who was short-listed for the Olympic team. Though she had her own facility near Aachen, she often traveled with her horses to Hilden in order to train with Balkenhol. Through him she managed to reach the top in international dressage competition.

A lazy horse must always be brought back to the basics—i.e. he must continually be worked toward achieving rhythm, suppleness and relaxation, and contact. In addition, the rider should try to find the causes of the horse's behavior. Has the horse always been lazy, or could he be developing an illness? Does his saddle fit correctly? Is the horse simply rather phlegmatic and sluggish by nature? If the horse is sick, the first order is to help him completely recover his health before returning to work. If, however, there are no health issues, the rider's priority should be to teach the horse to respond sensitively to the aids.

"Under no circumstances should the rider apply constant strong leg aids in order to drive his horse forward," warns Balkenhol, "because this will happen at the expense of expression, and will, in the long run, make the horse dull to the aids. Instead the rider should

When working a horse from the ground, Klaus Balkenhol applies the aids with the whip more energetically if necessary (left), followed immediately by aids that are finely dosed (right). (La Picolina ridden by the author, Britta Schöffmann.)

HORSES, HORSES, HORSES

In the meantime, Klaus Balkenhol had almost become a professional. He trained many horses after work on a daily basis, and took many up to Grand Prix. His daughter, Anabel, also now rode—taught primarily by her mother—at the highest levels of dressage. The family tradition was secure: all three Balkenhols were officially "crazy about horses."

ATLANTA

In 1995 Balkenhol and Goldie became European champions again and German champions for the fourth time. In 1996, the pair was again part of the Olympic team, this time headed for Atlanta, and Balkenhol was granted leave from his work in order to prepare for the Games. At this time, it also became clear that Balkenhol, now 57 years old, was considered a candidate for the job as coach of the German team.

Riding in a forward-and-downward stretched position is a key element in Balkenhol's training.

use a few leg aids that are 'more energetic'; if this is not enough, you should first apply the spurs, then possibly a tap with the whip in order to achieve the desired forward reaction from the horse. And when the horse does respond, he should be praised immediately so that he understands: 'Oh, I see! This is what my rider wants.' With time, the rider's aids can then become less and less significant. This is how the horse's basic impulsion—the basis for achieving expressive collection down the road—can be improved."

While Barcelona had been a particularly wonderful experience for the policeman, Atlanta turned out to be a little disappointing. Although success didn't fail to appear—he won a team gold medal and was sixth place in the individual scoring—the team's spirits were down. Balkenhol remembers: "Nadine Capellmann, who had bought Gracioso, was the reserve rider, and some people didn't like the fact that I was not only a team member but also her trainer, and on top of that, I was designated German team coach. Although I had great support from the top authorities in the German National Equestrian Federation, there were some riders who threw a wrench into my path. This made me very sad and still, to this day, casts a cloud over my memories of the Olympics in Atlanta."

Balkenhol believes that when working with allegedly "lazy" horses this approach is considerably more successful than employing unremitting forward driving aids every second of every step. "It's like a person who yells all the time," he says. "At some point, nobody will pay attention to him anymore. If, however, somebody who as a rule speaks very quietly suddenly raises his voice, he can be sure to receive everyone's attention. It's exactly this reaction that the rider wishes to have from his horse." Balkenhol does admit that horses with a natural desire to go forward are generally better suited for dressage. Either way, if a rider truly wants to develop impulsion, suppleness and relaxation is absolutely necessary. He says, "Impulsion, true impulsion, exists only in combination with suppleness. Everything else is riding for show and is not in accordance with the classical principles."

To recognize "true" impulsion is one thing, to maintain or improve it another. At Balkenhol's facility, horses are given as much time as they need to develop impulsion. If a four-year-old moves with decent impulsion yet still lacks a little bit of expression—who cares? In Balkenhol's opinion, impulsion can only be improved through continuous gymnasticization, the gaining of strength, and increased "letting through" of the aids. "A horse must first be in the position, physically as well as mentally, to present his natural impulsion in such a way that it appears to have more expression," says Balkenhol. "This is only possible when the horse is able to 'carry' himself. The frenzied 'running around' we

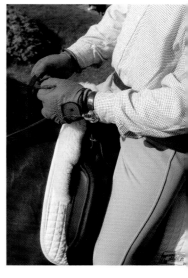

A horse must remain sensitive as this allows him to react to the finest of aids.

HIS OWN FACILITY

After the Olympic Games Balkenhol returned home—a home that was once more marked by moving preparations. The family had found a farm in Rosendahl, only a few miles away from Balkenhol's hometown, Velen.

The residential house of the Balkenhol family is in a style that's typical for farms in the Münsterland region.

currently see in many of the tests for three- and four-year-old horses in Germany, for example, doesn't make any sense to me."

His Highness, by Hohenstein, was a horse that was brought along very diligently and patiently from the beginning of his training. The stunningly beautiful black stallion was champion of the stallion licensing in Verden, Germany, in 2002. Purchased soon after by Doug and Louise Leatherdale, he was then entrusted to Balkenhol for training. His Highness had three exceptional basic gaits and a lot of natural impulsion. "Sure, if you added some pressure here and some more over there, you might have been able to tease out of His Highness some considerably more spectacular movements," Balkenhol admits. "But this was not what we wanted to do since it would only have been a short-term display of superficial effects. I wanted to preserve the beautiful manner in which this horse naturally moved, and simply cultivate it, rather than overdo it and thereby destroy it."

The frenzied running around we currently see in many of the tests for three- and four-year-old horses in Germany, for example, doesn't make any sense to me.

Those who observed the development of this horse over the weeks and months understood what Balkenhol meant. You could see how much His Highness enjoyed his movement—as did every rider who sat in his saddle! Every step the black stallion took was full of springiness and almost seemed to be "sucking" his rider into the saddle. "This is exactly what true and natural impulsion is," Balkenhol raves. "As opposed to artificially created 'hovering' steps, which are actually uncomfortable for the rider, sitting on a correctly swinging horse can be like sitting on a cloud—or like sitting on His Highness."

In Rosendahl, Balkenhol's dream of operating his own facility came true. The farm included 25 stalls, an indoor arena, and a 60-meter outdoor arena surrounded by pastures, fields, and woods. Until everything was ready to move, his horses stayed at the DOKR (German Olympic Committee of Riding) in Warendorf.

Balkenhol's indoor arena and outdoor ring are literally right in front of his living room window.

Sadly, the rising star faded too soon. The exceptional stallion, who had already produced ten approved sons in his first year of breeding, broke his right hock in a breeding accident at the end of April 2007 and had to be euthanized. His passing was a terrible loss to his owners, the breeding world, and the sport of dressage.

Of course not all horses have springy impulsion like this exceptional stallion did, and what impulsion they do have may have been "turned off" by incorrect work. Is this reason to despair? "Of course

From the forward-and-downward stretching position (left) a horse should allow himself to be shortened until the rider has reached a suitable working position (right) and vice versa, at any time.

ENDING A CAREER IN MÜNSTER

Balkenhol now took office as coach of the German dressage team. He took his new commitment very seriously. In order to do it justice, he quit his own show career, and decided to only work as a trainer. Inevitably, Goldstern's career as a dressage star was over. Atlanta was his last show—and a little later his "boss" rode his last Grand Prix test. In Münster, the town where his

On Garçon, Klaus Balkenhol celebrated his last victory.

not," Balkenhol says comfortingly. "It is true that not all horses have the same potential when it comes to impulsion. Some horses have more, others less. Nadine Capellmann's mount, Elvis, for instance, is a horse with quite an enormous amount of natural impulsion and extremely active hind legs. But even horses that have average gaits can, despite their limitations, be worked in such a way they can appear to have more 'swing'—that is, unless they're named Oleander, of course!"

BALKENHOL'S RECIPE FOR IMPULSION

- ▶ Don't upset a young horse's balance by riding too forward.
- ▶ On the other hand, don't "step on the brakes" all the time either.
- ▶ Always keep the horse sensitive to the forward driving aids.
- ▶ Focus the horse's concentration on the rider by alternately lengthening and shortening the steps.
- ▶ School the horse to accept the rider's finest, most delicate hand influence.
- ▶ Build the horse's ability for self-carriage by riding lateral movements, half-halts, and otherwise getting the hindquarters more under him.
- ▶ Later on in the training process the collected exercises and resulting increased ability in the horse to step under himself (and gain of strength) enables the rider to improve the horse's impulsion even more.

breakthrough to the top of competitive dressage took place, Balkenhol won the gold medal on the black stallion, Garçon, who he had also trained.

Impressive: "Goldie's" last dance to the sound of castanets.

STRAIGHTENING—
A NEVER-ENDING STORY

If you've ever been lucky enough to sit on a horse that has been ridden and trained by Klaus Balkenhol, you know how it feels when a horse is truly straight. Riding is equally comfortable in both directions. The quality of the movements to the left is just as good as to

Perfectly straight one-tempi changes are the result of years of correct work. (Aragon ridden by Guenter Seidel.)

GOODBYE "GOLDIE"

Goldstern stayed with Balkenhol and officially retired in 1999. The Interior Minister of North-Rhine Westphalia gave the former star to chief officer Balkenhol, who had retired early from the police service while getting his full pension. The audience bid Goldie farewell at Equitana in Essen—one last ride accompanied by the sound of castanets, one last time to thunderous applause.

Goldstern says goodbye at Equitana in Essen.

A horse's natural crookedness can transfer all the way to the poll if the rider applies incorrect aids, causing the horse to twist in his poll.

the right—without exceptions, without weaknesses, without one-sided stiffness. It makes you feel good. Achieving this goal, however, requires a lot of work and, above all, a lot of know-how. The fact that every horse is crooked by nature is by now something every child probably knows—at least every child who rides. Dealing with this crookedness, however, and attempting to diminish or eliminate it altogether causes even many good and experienced riders difficulty.

"The way one tackles the crookedness problem depends on the horse's age," Balkenhol says. "In young horses crookedness and lack of balance are closely interrelated. In older horses the crookedness has affected the muscle development in such a way that it's really difficult to make such horses straight again. In either case, a huge mistake is to try to make the horse straighter by using force and physical strength. It is the consistent, subtle, corrective measures—which often take place unconsciously in the background of the training process—of a good and experienced rider that leads to success."

When working with the horses in his care, Balkenhol only asks for as much forwardness as the horse is able to translate into his movement while staying as straight as possible. "Young horses are not yet strong in their hindquarters," he explains. "When moving forward at the trot, especially under the rider, they often can't lift their front feet off the ground quickly enough while the hind legs are reaching forward. If they are a bit crooked at the same time, they simply have to evade sideways with their hindquarters in order to avoid striking

Goldie spent his retirement years at Balkenhol's facility. He was turned out, ridden daily, and could still perform his entire program until his last days. On June 22, 2003, he died from the consequences of intestinal torsion at 22 years old.

FROM GERMANY TO AMERICA

Klaus Balkenhol remained coach of the German team for four years, collecting gold medals at two European Championships, one World Championship, and at the Olympic Games. But his task wore him out, especially because of all the quarrels he faced. As before, he continued to train his student, Nadine Capellmann, a situation not everybody approved of. Balkenhol was their front legs with their hind legs. So, if the rider asks for too forward a trot, instead of eliminating the horse's crookedness, he actually adds to it."

As usual, in order to correct a horse's natural crookedness one must have confirmed the other prerequisite components of the Training Scale. Rhythm, suppleness and relaxation, and also impulsion must have become such solid qualities that the horse begins to develop the necessary balance and strength for achieving the straightness strived for.

"As I've gained a lot of experience over the course of years, and because the riders I train all ride at a high level, the problem of crookedness, for the most part, isn't such a drastic one for me anymore," admits Balkenhol. "However, it must never be underestimated, even in highly trained horses. Goldstern, for instance, had a very pronounced natural crookedness in the beginning of our work together. When working with him, I always had to be aware of it and proceed quite deliberately. If at times I wasn't consistent, problems quickly crept in—in dressage tests this might well have manifested in mistakes in the flying changes. My first successful horse, Rabauke, was very crooked. When he was young, this even caused him to occasionally move so crookedly he almost was a little lame."

The fact that the chestnut became a successful Grand Prix horse despite his innate crookedness was due to his rider's deft way of correcting his problem slowly, and always without the use of force.

In the beginning Rabauke was so crooked that he leaned extremely into turns.

As German team coach, Klaus Balkenhol celebrated many great successes. From the left: Isabell Werth, Klaus Balkenhol, Alexandra Simons-de Ridder, Dr. Uwe Schulten-Baumer, Nadine Capellmann, chairman of the dressage committee Anton Fischer, and Ulla Salzgeber.

Balkenhol worked Rabauke a lot on the left hand, counter-flexed through the corners. "Only after some time did his muscles become strong enough so one could get him straighter and gradually ride him through turns with correct flexion and bend," he remembers. It

Getting a horse straight cannot be achieved by using force but only by influencing him subtly and consistently.

Klaus Balkenhol subtly asks His Highness with his inside hand to flex a little in the poll.

accused of having conflicts of interest. "All the politics that went on behind my back was simply not up my alley," he sums up today. At the end of 2000, he quit his job as German coach, exasperated.

However, there was no time for an early retirement. Balkenhol had never been more in demand than he was at this point. He received enquiries from abroad almost daily, one of which came from the US to coach their dressage team and help bring them to the top of the sport.

Nearly a year after the turn of the millennium, Balkenhol signed a contract with the United States Equestrian Federation. "The prospect of meeting new people and foreign countries as well as the challenge to help a country develop their equestrian team, to make it stronger, appealed to me," he explains.

took a whole year of work before Rabauke was able to go through corners not only straight in his body, but also evenly.

Balkenhol believes it's tremendously important to go through a preliminary phase of riding in counter-flexion when working with horses that are stiff on one side and unbalanced. What Waldemar Seunig's (1887–1976) book *Am Pulsschlag der Reitkunst* ("the pulse of horsemanship") had once taught a young knowledge-hungry Balkenhol can also be observed in horses at liberty. "Watch a horse cantering around the indoor arena without a rider," advises Balkenhol. "The faster he moves and the greater his balance problems are, the more he will look toward the outside in the corners to regain his balance."

It took a whole year before Rabauke was able to go through turns while remaining straight in his body and secure in his rhythm.

Merely flexing a horse to the outside isn't enough, though. What's more important is that the horse—when it's counter-flexed—also yields in the poll. "When the rider 'takes' on the left rein, for example, the horse must learn that he must flex to the left, become soft, and carry himself for a moment, thereby straightening," Balkenhol explained while demonstrating on His Highness. The stallion responded immediately to his rider's aids, flexing and bending evenly to the right or left, depending on his rider's request. "The secret," Balkenhol says, "lies in correct yielding of the rein. It must happen exactly at the moment when the horse yields—even if it's only for a moment. This is how he will learn to carry himself. Most people make the mistake of either moving their hand forward too early (before the horse has yielded), or they wait too long and do not allow

LIKE A WORLD CHAMPION

The life of Balkenhol changed once again. Instead of enjoying the quiet everyday life as a trainer at his own facility, Balkenhol now packed suitcases and flew across the "big pond." On the side he still trained

Employing scrutinizing eyes, Klaus Balkenhol now gives directions from the trainer's chair.

the horse to carry himself and thereby straighten."

In Balkenhol's opinion, the biggest mistake made in the attempt to achieve straightness is the use of physical strength or force. "One cannot pull or force a horse to be straight," he says emphatically. "This only causes tension and develops the wrong muscles, thereby worsening one-sided crookedness in the long run. Instead, the rider should always keep the expression 'gymnasticization' in mind. Gymnasticization is not bodybuilding. Only if the horse evenly develops— in terms of mobility and strength—the muscles on both sides of his body can he, within his straightness, execute all movements in both directions well and without restraint."

Problems in piaffe, passage, or flying changes are often caused by a lack of straightness.

Crooked horses can be seen everywhere, more so at the lower levels than the upper ones. But even in the latter an experienced observer will easily be able to spot a horse that isn't straight. It may not be sideways or evasive steps that betray his crookedness, but rather his poor performance of more difficult movements. As Balkenhol asserts, "All horses that have problems in the piaffe-passage transitions, that have an uneven passage, or that tend to make mistakes in the flying changes, have problems with straightness."

Nadine Capellmann (among others), who had become a multiple-time German champion on Gracioso and had another top horse in the barn with Farbenfroh. He learned English bit by bit, applying the principle, "learning by doing," and thoroughly enjoyed working with the American riders. In partic-

Klaus Balkenhol and his star pupil, Nadine Capellmann.

An expressive extension at the trot, such as that seen here, requires that a horse is straight.

ular he liked the camaraderie among the US riders. "In America riders are not jealous about other people's success," he explains, "but are instead happy for them. They sincerely acknowledge success—even the success of competitive rivals."

Balkenhol gave regular clinics in the US, forming individual riders and horses as well as a powerful national team. His facility in Rosendahl became a training camp for American riders. The riders felt comfortable in Rosendahl and were fully behind their coach. His wife, Judith, organized in the background, buying airplane tickets, taking care of visas and accommodation, planning itineraries, and handling minor emergencies.

In 2002, in Jerez de la Frontera, Spain, it happened: for the first time in the history of American dressage sport, a US team (Debbie McDonald, Guenter Seidel, Sue Blinks, and Lisa Wilcox) won a silver medal at the World Champi-

FROM COLLECTION TO DANCING

Expressive and relaxed collected work shows that the rider has understood the steps that led up to it.

During his time as an active competitor, Klaus Balkenhol had his greatest successes with his police horse, Goldstern, the "small chestnut with the big potential." The pair not only won almost every honor available, they also became revered champions of the Freestyle. For years "Goldie" danced to the sounds of castanets—percussion instruments consisting of two small shells of hard wood, ivory, or plastic fastened to and clicked together by a dancer's fingers—featured in fiery, Spanish music. The fact that this music matched the horse so well was not only thanks to perfect arrangement—it was also due to Goldstern's ability to collect with the highest cadence and react to the slightest cue from his rider while still remaining relaxed and supple. Because of this, the pair seemed to float through their Freestyle effortlessly. Such a performance is only possible if the rider has taken the time in his training of the horse to establish the necessary foundation for "true" collection.

"Collection is attained via all the previous work one has done based on the Training Scale," Balkenhol emphasizes. "Collected work that looks expressive, loose, and playful confirms the rider and horse have understood the previous steps. We want to achieve collection as a result of having worked with the horse systematically—in other words, we want collection that enables more cadence and loftiness

onships and put three riders in the top ten. This was a success such as had never been seen before. At the same time, Balkenhol's success as a trainer reached another high: His top student, Nadine Capellmann, won the team and individual gold medal riding Farbenfroh.

OLYMPICS AND SADNESS

The success of the American team boosted the sport of dressage on the other side of the Atlantic. Little by little the American team turned into a strong competitor in the battle for international championship titles and medals.

With his top private student, however, Balkenhol had bad luck. Nadine Capellmann's mount, Farbenfroh, injured himself and dropped out of the spotlight for a

In the course of his career, Goldstern developed a piaffe-passage tour that demonstrated the lightness of a dancer.

long time. A comeback attempt failed and the exceptional chestnut never really found his way back to his old form. He remained in poor health for years and finally suffered a femoral neck fracture when regaining consciousness in the recovery stall after a minor operation. Only fourteen, Farbenfroh had to be euthanized in the Olympic year of 2004, a few days before Christmas.

In the same year, at the Olympic Games in Athens, Balkenhol led his US riders (Debbie McDonald, Robert Dover, Guenter Seidel, and Lisa Wilcox) on to win the bronze medal.

An optimal extension can only be developed if the horse can carry himself during collection. (Rocher ridden by US rider, George Williams.)

through the strength and endurance of the hindquarters via the horse's back. What some riders believe is collection—say, the 'hovering' steps encouraged in young horses and geared toward impressing an audience—is merely a sham in my opinion. And to make matters worse, it is done at the expense of the horse, whose health will suffer sooner or later."

THE SEPARATION

Balkenhol continued to train his student, Nadine Capellmann, working with her, her young prospects, as well as some newly acquired horses. At her trainer's urging, Capellmann sent her naughty youngster, Elvis, to profes-

A winning team for thirteen years: Klaus Balkenhol and Nadine Capellmann went their separate ways in 2005.

Alternating between high collection and extension furthers the horse's ability to "step forward," and the strength in the horse's hindquarters.

When Balkenhol rides or teaches he always makes sure that the collected work meets his requirements in all three basic gaits. In the collected walk he wants to see lofty, active, forward steps in a clear four-beat rhythm and a horse that carries himself and is light in the hand. He doesn't want to see a "blurry, slow fumbling of the legs." In the collected trot and canter he desires cadenced steps where the forward impulse is clearly visible with the horse's nose approaching the vertical, and the poll the highest point.

"The quality of collected work often shows up very well in the extensions, especially at the trot," Balkenhol explains. "It's quite strenuous work for a horse to carry himself with increased forward momen-

The quality of a horse's collection is also shown in his extensions.

sional rider, Heiner Schiergen. The young horse liked to buck and had already made three Olympic riders hit the sand—the risk of an injury before the World Championships was too great.

"I trained Nadine for thirteen years," Balkenhol says, "and it has filled me with great joy to accompany her on the way to the top of international dressage. The USEF wasn't thrilled about the fact that I trained a German, of course (who then also has become a two-time World champion), but I always explained that I owed it to Nadine and our long-time collaboration."

In 2005 this long and extremely successful cooperation came apart when Nadine Capellmann got involved with Martin Schaudt. He wanted to take over the training of her horses—an arrangement that didn't last long.

Gracioso and Klaus Balkenhol demonstrating the highest degree of collection and harmony.

IN WORLDWIDE DEMAND

Klaus Balkenhol has hardly had time to show his disappointment. The demand to train with him is too great. His idyllic farm in Rosendahl has become a point of reference for national and international names in dressage sport. In addition, he travels often to the US to coach the American dressage team and all over the world to lecture on the topic of "classical dressage training." And of course, there's his passion to ride.

To this day the master rides every day, working his own horses, which his daughter Anabel shows successfully. He still rides his students' horses in order to feel, correct, and briefly show his riders how "it's supposed to look."

tum while covering a lot of ground and slightly stretching his neck. It only works if the collection in itself is correct.

"In this respect the expression 'lengthening the frame' is very important to me. It doesn't mean that the horse only lengthens his neck. If this happens, the horse's hindquarters haven't gained enough strength for collected work yet. A neck that has been made short through hand influence (something that, sadly, all too many riders and judges have grown accustomed to accepting over the last few years) also demonstrates a lack of collection. A horse can only 'swing forward' as much as his frame allows him to—if he's pulled together by the rider's hands, he might throw his front legs in a spectacular way, but there's no 'swinging' in his back whatsoever."

The horses Balkenhol rides and trains all swing through their backs. If they get tense, he immediately takes a step back toward the basics instead of squeezing out some pseudo-impulsion and pseudo-collection by applying more pressure. "When it comes to collection, it must be joyful for both horse and rider," he claims. "Only then will it turn into a dance." Both Gracioso and Goldstern were superb athletes who, at the height of their careers, were able to perform this dance almost playfully. "Once they understood what collection was, they were able to perform perfectly," Balkenhol remembers. "I would guess there was hardly a horse who did more exact, more powerful, and more beautiful piaffe-passage transitions

Riding Gracioso in his piaffe-passage tour was something very special.

Klaus Balkenhol on His Highness.

Little Big Man under Anabel Balkenhol with a lofty collection.

than Gracioso. To ride him in these movements—that was quite an extraordinary experience. It was harmony in its purest form."

This same feeling was also gained from Anabel Balkenhol's one-time prospect, Little Big Man. The elastic bay gelding was able to

MORE MEDALS

Led by Klaus Balkenhol, the US dressage team is still on the road to success. At the World Equestrian Games in Aachen in 2006, the team won the bronze medal, and in the Grand Prix Special individual scoring Steffen Peters achieved a superb fourth place—another reward for all their hard work.

"It always makes me happy to see how well the American riders get along with each other and sup- port each other," Balkenhol says with a smile.

And it won't come as a surprise to anyone that around the champi- onships there are lots of parties. After all, riding, all of us agree, is supposed to be fun!

translate his big forward movement into expressively carried uphill movement seemingly without any effort at all. Unfortunately, disease brought an early end to this exceptional talent. Only nine years old at the time, "Litti" was diagnosed with colon cancer—a few weeks before he was to show in his first Grand Prix.

In order to develop a horse's ability to collect, and perfect his willingness to collect, Balkenhol strictly follows the classical principles. Apart from the "time factor," which every horse is granted depending on individual physical and mental development, this again means for Balkenhol: Training Scale, Training Scale, Training Scale. "Only by following the Training Scale will a rider achieve the suppleness and relaxation, which—despite the necessary 'positive' body tension—should emanate from the horse in all collected movements," he insists.

When maintaining and schooling the collected movements, Balkenhol always makes sure—both in his role as rider and coach—that the understanding of the aids is continually being refined in both horse and rider. For this reason, he asks for half-halts in all basic gaits and at all tempos, again and again. "The rider must learn to aid subtly, and the horse must learn to respond subtly," he says. "Only when the horse balances himself through the half-halts can he collect, and once at his most athletic form, perform piaffe and passage."

Regardless of all his necessary positive body tension, the horse should always emanate looseness and suppleness.

Beaming after their success at the World Championships in Aachen: Guenter Seidel, Debbie McDonald, Steffen Peters, Leslie Morse, and Klaus Balkenhol.

THE SECRET: PREPARATION AND TIME

Among experts, Klaus Balkenhol has a reputation as "the king" of piaffe-passage. In addition, other difficult upper-level movements are his strength—precisely because he always envisions the classical training principles. "For me, a correct piaffe or an expressive passage are always the result of correct training," he says. "Often, it is these movements, in particular, that are practiced prematurely, thereby leading to a dead end and resulting in resistance. Or a horse might simply forever execute the movement incorrectly."

Piaffe and passage are often practiced too early in a horse's training.

What one sees in the world's most prestigious show arenas speaks volumes: hurried piaffes with the front legs positioned too far forward or too far back as a means of support; front or hind legs evading sideways; unnatural "jerking" up of the legs; rhythm faults in the passage; dragging hind legs; and bumpy transitions. One rarely sees a really classically beautiful (and correct) piaffe and passage. "Most of the time, mistakes were made at some point on the way to achieving these movements, which the horse then somehow compensates for," Balkenhol explains. "A very experienced and good rider, and/or instructor is required to recognize problems at an early stage and correct or prevent them. This is tremendously important since mistakes in training will affect the rider's own abilities—some immediately, others only years later. Once the rider has practiced certain movements incorrectly, they are very difficult to correct."

Training mistakes will always come back to haunt the rider— sometimes even years later.

Le Bo, Carola Koppelmann's top mount, was a case of a "piaffe problem." He had developed the habit of stepping sideways with his hind legs instead of remaining properly on one track. At the same time, he placed his front legs too far forward for support, the result being that his back wasn't able to "carry." He had simply learned the piaffe incorrectly—probably at a time when he hadn't yet developed enough carrying power in his haunches. By stepping sideways, the smart chestnut "faked" balance in the piaffe, and this faulty movement became so second nature to him that he wasn't able to let go of it even after he had developed sufficient physical strength.

Anabel Balkenhol's mare, Easy, also had problems with the piaffe. A beautiful bay that came to the Balkenhol's as a five-year-old, she

If you take your time, almost everything will work out in the end.

had obviously been taught her first piaffe steps incorrectly and with too much pressure, which had created tension and anxiety in the mare and caused her to brace with her front legs and respond with explosive temper outbursts. For a while even Balkenhol doubted whether he would be able to solve Easy's problems. Five years later her piaffe was outstanding. "It just took a long time," Balkenhol says with a cheerful grin. "If you take the time, almost everything will work out in the end."

Well, time might have been a factor indeed, but only to a certain degree. The king of piaffe's secret also lies in his ability to tune into each individual horse and related potential problems, to solve each

Klaus Balkenhol—here riding the stallion, Kingston— is considered a specialist in piaffe and passage.

problem individually, and to stimulate the necessary impulse in the hindquarters. "Le Bo lost his balance because his hind legs became too slow in the piaffe," Balkenhol explains. "So we made an effort to first get him to accept half-halts from a very light hand while raising his feet more quickly behind and—very importantly—thereby lifting his back." Balkenhol chose transitions and shoulder-ins to encourage the chestnut to "swing" in balance toward the hands, and to revive the impulse from behind while maintaining a constant forward tendency. When collecting him, he asked for a few quick steps instead of many slow (and bad) ones. Gradually Le Bo stopped swaying— evident of his sideways evasion—in the piaffe. With his increasingly

The mare, Easy, now a Grand Prix winner, initially had a hard time with the piaffe.

solid performance at Grand Prix level, he and his rider even managed the jump onto the Olympic long list.

Easy, too, eventually turned into a successful Grand Prix horse—despite all the bad signs in the beginning. "With her we embarked on a different path, like with Debbie McDonald's mare, Brentina," says Balkenhol. "Normally one should teach a horse the piaffe first, and only then the passage, since it's generally easier for horses to lift their feet diagonally on the spot than remain suspended longer while the hind legs swing forward. But as exceptions prove to be the rule, as everyone knows, and since one must never forget that all horses are individuals, with Easy I chose the opposite approach.

Never forget that all horses are individuals!

"I first schooled and perfected the passage, then began the piaffe again. The more solid and supple she became during the passage, the less nervous she'd become when I directed her collection a little more toward the piaffe. This way she learned on a mental level that she didn't have to run away from anything and that she always had an open door through which she could escape: the passage. Step by step she accepted the aids for the piaffe without losing her mind and balance. Today when I see her perform a relaxed, happy piaffe, my heart overflows with joy."

BALKENHOL'S GRAND PRIX TIPS
DEVELOPING, IMPROVING, ELIMINATING FAULTS: IMPULSION

Regardless of the movement or gait one is riding in, what I find highly important is impulsion, that is, the energetic translation of power from the hindquarters over the working back toward the front of the horse. Without this nothing much will happen, especially not in the realms of higher collection and difficult movements.

I always distinguish between a horse's innate impulsion—based on character and personality, willingness to cooperate, and forward desire—and the impulsion created and maintained by the rider's motivation. If the horse has no or hardly any natural impulsion, I as the

Impulsion must always come from actively working hind legs (top); hooves that are dragging in the sand are a sign of a lack of impulsion (bottom).

rider have to continually ask my horse to cooperate, which isn't always a pleasure. If the horse does have natural impulsion, however, it's the rider's most important duty to foster and cultivate it, not stifle it. In my opinion, one can only foster and cultivate it through positive training experiences. The rider must always try to ensure that the horse enjoys his work. Other than correct riding, this is achieved by frequently praising the horse and understanding his needs. Riding outside the arena, free schooling, gymnastic jumping—all this can motivate a horse and not only preserve his natural impulsion but even further it. If such management is paired with clear aids and sensitive responses to the horse, one will be able to ride with extremely fine aiding in the long run—which is both a goal as well as the prerequisite for permanently preserving the horse's impulsion.

If, however, impulsion has been lost in the course of training, be it through incorrect riding, harsh training techniques, or maybe due to a horse's illness, it can take a very, very long time to revive it. To be successful the rider must, again, look for the underlying causes, as is so often the case. He must ask himself: Have I worked the horse too much? Have I done too much piaffe? Is my horse mentally overwhelmed? Are my horse's muscles sore? An experienced rider will

"Our families have known each other for a very long time. This came in handy, of course, when I was looking for a dressage trainer who would be able to help me with my very difficult Thoroughbred, Watermill Stream. Klaus was the trainer who showed me that an event horse can have a "big trot," too, and how to teach it to (often difficult) Thoroughbreds. What I learned at that time more than helps me today with all my students, and certainly plays a big part in all the medals and victories I've won over the last few years."

BETTINA HOY
Event rider, Olympian, team World Cup medalist, European champion, multiple-time German champion.

notice what's wrong, and adjust his actions accordingly. Conversely, an inexperienced rider often reacts incorrectly and tries to force the horse in some way. These are the typical moments when people say: "I must ride him through this." Pressure at the wrong moment, however, leads to a loss of impulsion and subsequently to the deterioration of the horse's entire performance, but especially the difficult movements. In order to prevent such a problem, the rider must understand his horse, listen to him carefully, and act quickly. A horse will begin to complain only after a long period of suffering.

DEVELOPING, IMPROVING, ELIMINATING FAULTS: PIAFFE

Piaffe characteristics of different horses: Aragon ridden by US team rider, Guenter Seidel...

Almost any horse can be taught to piaffe. The quality of the individual piaffe, however, can be quite different from horse to horse as it depends on a variety of factors: the horse's conformation, his talent, his nerves, and also the skill of his rider, of course. Horses, for instance, with extremely long backs or hindquarters that are too angulated often tend to have a harder time with the piaffe. Horses with a long back lack the ability to get under their center of gravity, and horses with an extreme angulation in the hindquarters often step so far forward during the piaffe they lose their balance.

Years ago I had a long discussion with Willi Schultheis about what's more favorable for a good piaffe—hind legs that are rather straight or hind legs with strong angulation. We both came to the conclusion that horses with extremely angled hindquarters have a harder time.

Also, horses that are extremely nervous or particularly lazy and sluggish often have difficulties with this movement. Therefore, when choosing a horse, I always make sure that he naturally has the right conformation and disposition, that is, a correct build with active hindquarters, a well-formed back, and an even-tempered character that likes to learn.

Only ask for the first piaffe steps, which really are not more than very short reprises of half steps, when the horse—provided he has been worked according to the Training Scale—is physically and mentally strong enough and responds extremely sensitively to half-halts.

...La Picolina ridden by author, Britta Schöffmann (the mare is "sitting" well in the piaffe)...

...and Rocher under US rider, George Williams (note the forearm springs correctly onto a horizontal line).

This isn't necessarily a question of the horse's age but the degree of his maturity and what he offers voluntarily. A young horse can respond in such a rideable way and with so much suppleness that I might attempt half steps (diagonal stepping with the slightest forward movement). If the horse offers the first steps toward piaffe,

Only a correctly trained horse can master the change from the four-beat rhythm of the walk (left) into the two-beat rhythm of the piaffe (right) without any problems.

I accept and thoroughly praise him. But to demand this movement from a three- or four-year-old horse is nonsense. A horse of this age simply can't show true piaffe steps because his carrying power hasn't yet developed appropriately.

When preparing for the first piaffe steps, I like to use lateral movements, especially shoulder-in, travers, and renvers at the walk and trot. These movements improve the horse's carrying power because the respective inside hind leg is asked to carry more and track more narrowly. If you can work equally well in both directions with an even rhythm and without losing impulsion at the trot, then the first step toward the piaffe—no, it's really the second step because the half-halts combined with a prompt step forward are the first one—has been done. I also concentrate on alternating between increased carrying and pushing in trot-canter work. I finally ask for the first preparatory half steps by transitioning from collected trot to walk, then trot on again immediately, and again immediately ride a transition to walk.

This teaches the horse to react to the sustaining and forward driving aids in quick succession. Horses that are willing to learn often get a bit overeager, which might show up in a little jigging after the transition to walk—a reaction I reward the horse for immediately in this phase, since it really is exactly what I want: one or two diagonal steps with little forward movement. By driving with both legs in a pulsing manner at the same time, and light hands that play backward, I teach the horse to connect this aid with the half steps. In this phase it's extremely important to be content with very few steps. Even if it's only two or three steps initially, one should always praise the horse.

One never must ask for highly collected movements by using force. If too much pressure is put on the horse, tension and subsequently faulty motion sequences are the result. Such problems are very difficult to solve later on—if at all.

If, on the other hand, a horse has learned the first diagonal half steps and the aiding related to them—in other words, the horse has understood what I want from him—then I frequently and playfully include piaffe-like steps in my program. Initially I may allow just a few steps that are always forward-moving, then gradually ten or twelve steps—always only as many as the horse is physically and mentally ready and able to perform. After all, later on the piaffe must be a movement that radiates relaxed, lofty control, not hectic, forced stamping on the spot.

It's always important that a horse lifts his back in the piaffe, like a bridge between the forehand and hindquarters. The rider must prepare the horse for this with basic work. If mistakes were made along the way, and if the horse has a weak back or tends to sink it away from the rider, then the horse will have difficulty learning the piaffe. Conversely, if the horse has learned in the course of his training to take up more weight with his hindquarters in all the other collected movements, then it will be easier for him to learn the piaffe.

The quality of a piaffe undergoes different developmental stages. A horse that has just learned to piaffe will not be able to perform it as loftily as an older, well-trained horse, which from the strength in its hindquarters alone is able to perform steps on the spot, springing toward the rider's hand. For this reason one must beware demanding perfection in the early stages of piaffe training. Each horse needs his own timetable in order to master such a difficult movement. If difficulties arise along the way, I can only recommend taking a step back and again working on the basics: the horse's suppleness, half-halts, and sensitivity towards the aids.

Piaffe in different developmental stages: a dressage prospect at the beginning of piaffe training (top), and an experienced Grand Prix horse in beautiful self-carriage (bottom).

If, however, one is given a horse and mistakes have already been made, or have arisen despite all applied caution, there's a suitable remedy for (almost) every such case—although the result will probably not be as good as it would have been had the piaffe been optimally prepared for and taught. Keep in mind as you read this that the rider must never support the piaffe by using so much whip that the horse feels pain. Praise the horse every single time he does well instead—it is the latter method of training that will encourage the horse to gradually develop a piaffe characterized by lightness and easiness.

So, to continue: if a horse has problems with the piaffe, regardless of the type of problem, the cause most of the time is a lack of innate impulsion. A piaffe will only be successful if the horse performs it on his own from the lightest of aids. I act; the horse reacts. If the horse doesn't, perhaps because he has been pressured to perform and therefore reacts with tension, or with resigned insensitivity—in which case it's important to recreate both trust and sensitivity.

On the one hand, as I mentioned earlier, the rider will certainly have to work on the basics again, according to the Training Scale. On the other, I've realized that the easiest way to recreate impulsion—especially with horses that hardly react to a light leg aid or don't react to it at all—is to lengthen the reins (really long) and apply an energetic tap with the whip combined with a forward driving aid with both legs. This gives my horse the feeling that there's a door open in front of him for him to go through.

Conversely, when he drives energetically forward with the reins short, the rider puts pressure on the horse, which much of the time leads to tension and a counter-reaction. In such situations, horses tend to work against the whip aid instead of developing an understanding of the real aid and going forward as requested.

When schooling a horse in piaffe, the rider must never forget that this movement not only tests the quality of the basic work he has done with his horse, it also tests his riding and ability to influence the horse—every incorrect move on his part prevents his horse from performing a lofty, supple piaffe.

Klaus Balkenhol demonstrates different rider influences and their consequences:

The rider falls forward and lightens his seat too much, and the horse "sticks" to the ground, tenses his back, and leans against the reins.

The poll is too high, the horse is tense and evades the piaffe as he starts to lean on his legs, appearing discontent and tense.

Here, the poll is pulled in too tightly, the horse is tense, leans backward, pushes his hind legs out behind, and doesn't step in a clear diagonal sequence of footfalls.

Finally, the same horse is ridden correctly and performing a relaxed piaffe with his nose slightly in front of the vertical as he "swings" toward the rider's hand.

CORRECTING FAULTS IN THE PIAFFE

LEANING ON THE FRONT LEGS: This fault is most often created by collecting and stepping in place too early, before the horse is able to balance his weight on his hindquarters. Also, when the horse pushes his hind legs too far forward underneath his body, he may tend to lean on his front legs. In these cases I recommend focusing on riding forward half steps. Once the rider manages to ride these forward half steps with a light hand, it helps to alternate between two or three piaffe steps in place, and then these piaffe steps forward. This way the hindquarters are again engaged and the necessary impulsion returns.

EVADING SIDEWAYS—HIND LEGS: This problem is caused by a lack of balance and can be difficult to eliminate once the horse has internalized it. It can help to alternate between riding shoulder-in, travers, and renvers, combined with short reprises of piaffe steps in a shoulder-in position.

EVADING SIDEWAYS—FRONT LEGS: Once it has become a habit, this fault is difficult to correct, as well. Horses with this problem develop little impulsion from the hindquarters (too little forwardness), which is necessary for a piaffe to be performed in place. This fault often arises when the horse is pressured to perform difficult movements too early. I recommend a lot of lateral work, piaffe-like steps in a shoulder-fore position, in order to reestablish a connection to the hand and thereby achieve a correct contact. Correcting this problem can take a very long time!

UNEVEN STEPS: This is due to improper development of impulsion from the hindquarters. With a fourteen-year-old horse, the rider should ask himself if it's worthwhile making the effort to correct this fault—with an eight- or nine-year-old, however, a lot can still be achieved. First, return to the basics based on the Training Scale and determine if the horse has any physical weaknesses or if he is mentally overwhelmed. The rider must pay more attention to keeping the horse relaxed during collected work—both in trot and canter. In this way the horse's strength is also increased to better handle the highest degrees of collection.

DEVELOPING, IMPROVING, ELIMINATING FAULTS: PASSAGE

Unfortunately, riders make many mistakes when schooling the passage. The reason might be that it is possible to "squeeze" passage-like steps out of many horses by using strength and pressure. Such steps, however, are usually only "hovering," tense steps and lead to considerable problems in the long run since the horse excessively tightens his body and will feel pain sooner or later. These "hovering" steps arise from tiredness, and the horse leans, or "rests" on the rider's hands. This problem can be troublesome, especially if the rider thinks he is actually riding passage.

This incorrect movement is due to the horse leaning on the forehand and tightening the back rather than using carrying and pushing

In the passage the horse is supposed to "swing" powerfully forward-and-upward over his back.

I am completely against introducing young horses to the passage before they are ready.

"Klaus is very calm and always keeps track of everything. His absolute strength lies in the schooling of piaffe and passage, which he not only is able to teach to the horses well, but which he can ride exquisitely. He also tunes into both horse and rider. He doesn't have one method for every one and every horse, but individual solutions. This is also what makes his coaching for competition so special. Klaus always has a solution for any problem immediately. Excuses such as 'I don't know how to do that' are not in his lexicon."

NADINE CAPELLMANN

Two-time World champion, team Olympic medalist, multiple-time German champion

power that has been properly developed. A correct passage should feature forward springing hind legs and a "swinging" back. The rider mustn't forget that the back muscle is the biggest muscle in the horse's body, and when it is under stress, it is difficult to keep the blood circulating and providing an optimal supply of oxygen. Every tightening of the muscles, every tension limits blood circulation and oxygen distribution, which leads to sore muscles in the horse's back. For this reason alone, it must be the rider's absolute priority to preserve and better the "swinging" activity.

When schooling the passage, I make absolutely certain that the prolonged suspension phase of the trot—that's all the passage really is—truly stems from active hind legs. For this to happen, the rider must have strengthened the hind legs through his previous work with the horse. This is why I reject introducing young horses to the passage too early. Indeed, some horses may have a trot that already looks a little bit like a passage, but this is inherent in the gait and has no muscular basis—that is, it has not developed from an increase in hindquarter strength.

As I mentioned before, I develop this hindquarter strength in our horses through the basic exercises according to the Training Scale. It's very helpful to ride transitions within the trot, applying half-halts to achieve different tempos, as well as do lateral work.

Before schooling the passage, I generally school horses in piaffe. For most horses it's easier this way. If you begin with the passage, you run the risk of the horse misunderstanding the aids and trying to passage in place, which is impossible because the prolonged phase of suspension cannot be kept up and balance problems are sure to arise. If, on the other hand, you first school the piaffe, then you also increase the carrying power in the hindquarters as you train the horse to step actively off the ground and react willingly to the finest of aids—all prerequisites for a passage performed in self-carriage. There are always exceptions to the rule, of course. One must never try to proceed in a formulaic way, but be aware of each horse's individuality and adapt to it. Only the rider who understands this will ultimately succeed.

Moving on, if a horse has mastered the piaffe—or at least has some solid understanding of it—then I start at the trot and bring him back with my aids, and since he knows the signal for the piaffe, he'll

Before Klaus Balkenhol introduces a horse to the passage, he generally schools the piaffe.

react by lowering his haunches preparing for the transition. At exactly this very moment, I increase my forward driving aids again while at the same time intercepting the horse's move forward with more half-halts. A correctly ridden and halfway talented horse will—with an engaged hind leg—react by remaining in the suspension phase of the gait for a little longer since he doesn't know if his rider wishes him to go forward or not. He literally waits for his rider's aids. When the horse reacts in this way, I immediately praise him, signaling that he's done exactly what I expected from him by prolonging the airborne phase.

"First piaffe, then passage" is easier for most horses.

Since a horse needs an enormous amount of strength and conditioning for this exercise, early in his training he'll only be able to

In order to teach the horse his first passage steps, Klaus Balkenhol brings him back from the trot until he almost piaffes ...

perform very few passage steps. The art of riding consists of sensing when the horse loses his strength—in this case, when to ride forward again. If the rider pushes the horse beyond this point, he forces the horse to use muscles other than those in his hindquarters to push the body upward and "hold" the airborne moment. It's like a person lifting a heavy burden from the ground by bending over and pulling up with his back rather than squatting down and lifting from the legs— which would be the correct way to do it.

In order to transition correctly from the collected trot into the passage, the rider must make sure he uses only light rein aids and the horse has actively forward springing hind legs as well as a lifted back. If the horse happens to get tense, I ride these transitions while turning because in turns, the inside hind leg has to take up more weight anyway, and it also helps me supple the horse. If this doesn't work, I take a step back and work again on half-halts and the horse's sensitivity toward the aids.

The passage must develop gradually, just like the piaffe. "Expression"

...then rides more forward again, while at the same time intercepting the forward motion.

and longer passage series can be achieved only when the horse gains strength and thoroughly understands the rider's aids. Here, as everywhere else, the rider will only be successful if he fulfills the demands of the Training Scale: rhythm, in this case a clear two-beats, must be correct; the horse should be mentally and physically relaxed and supple, despite the necessary "positive body tension"; he should move forward full of impulsion; and he should be straight with an even, light contact.

If the quality of the horse's straightness is in question, the passage often has a "swaying" motion to it or there are uneven steps, since crookedness comes at the expense of balance. If the rider tries to fix this issue by applying one-sided leg aids and one-sided sustaining rein aids, he only aggravates the problem. Instead, he should take a step back and work on the basics again—as is so often necessary in dressage training. In this case, the means for success lies in riding on bent lines, applying half-halts, strengthening and gymnasticizing the horse on both sides, and improving the horse's "throughness."

Sometimes the only solution is to go back to the basics.

The path to mastering the passage is a long one: a young horse at a loose working trot(top), a seven-year-old learning the passage (middle), and finally, a nine-year-old entering the Grand Prix level (bottom). One can clearly see the differences in each horse's carrying power.

CORRECTING FAULTS IN THE PASSAGE

"HOVERING" STEPS: If this is an issue, the rider must improve the impulsion from the horse's hindquarters. This can only be done by going back to the basics in order to reestablish connection: hind legs—horse's back—rider's hand. In such cases I work the horse forward and try to make his hind legs step more quickly and energetically. This can be achieved by alternating between short phases of collection and extension at the trot and canter (no "running"!) Improving the horse's strength along with establishing a better contact must be the rider's priority.

DRAGGING HIND LEGS: What's usually lacking here is again the horse's innate impulsion. Until the problem becomes apparent, the rider has likely settled for too little impulsion. In these cases, I sometimes work the horse in hand, and support the horse with the whip during the passage. When applied at the right moment, it prompts the horse to swing his hind legs further and more actively under his center of gravity. From the saddle the rider must refine his aids, between the light, momentary impulses with his legs and a cleverly sustaining and yet yielding hand. This is the only way he can prevent the horse's hindquarters from "blocking up" again.

INDISTINCT PHASE OF SUSPENSION: Remaining suspended for a period of time requires a great amount of strength from the horse. If this is lacking, the horse will be unable to keep up the high degree of collection necessary for the passage. In this case the rider mainly has to work on strengthening the horse, which can be achieved by riding all kinds of transitions. What's also crucial here is improving impulsion so the hind legs swing actively through and so the horse's back can carry better. As always, if necessary, go back to the basics!

SWAYING: This fault is generally a sign of poor balance and also a lack of forward strength and impulsion. Horses that tend to sway should be ridden more forward during the passage, until they are better able to keep their balance. The swaying will gradually disappear.

UNEVEN ACTION IN THE HIND LEGS: This is a fault that's quite difficult to eliminate if it has existed for a long period of time, and it can appear in both the passage and the piaffe. In both cases, it is usually a sign of the horse having been overfaced when he was young, or of a rider always applying the whip on one side of the horse's body. I work to correct this fault the same in both the passage and the piaffe, with shoulder-fore, alternating short passage series in both directions and also in turns, and if necessary, with more forwardness.

DEVELOPING, IMPROVING, ELIMINATING FAULTS: PIAFFE-PASSAGE TRANSITIONS

Transitions between piaffe and passage can be particularly difficult. Horses that have a problem with one or both exercises often cannot perform the transitions without constraint and tension. Most horses are better at moving from the passage to the piaffe than vice versa. This is probably simply because it doesn't require as much strength as does moving out of the piaffe in place into the sustained suspension of the passage.

My introduction of these transitions to younger horses naturally develops out of previous work. In other words, I don't first teach the horse the piaffe, then the passage, and finally the transition between the two. Instead, one movement always merges somewhat into the other. This merging begins with the first half-way successful piaffe steps, which I then fade more and more frequently into a collected trot. The same applies to the reverse transition: beginning in a collected trot, I keep driving the horse—now quite familiar with half steps, or piaffe steps as the case may be—to hold the movement for two or three steps during the downward transition to walk or halt, all

The transition from piaffe (top) into passage (right) will be successful only if the horse has enough strength, "throughness," and sensitivity.

the while making sure that the horse understands my aids and reacts sensitively to them.

I use a similar approach as soon as the horse has learned his first passage steps. I include the "transition into" and the "transition out of" the movement quite casually in our work. After all, at some point along the line I'd like to be able to promptly and fluidly transition from walk, trot, or piaffe into a passage. Since it's easier for most horses to learn the passage from a collected trot, it's generally the exercise I start out with. Here, the better the horse reacts to my aids, remaining in the passage for gradually longer periods of time, the stronger his haunches become—a natural prerequisite for developing the passage from the walk. The walk-passage transition is particularly difficult because the horse must switch instantly from a four-beat rhythm to a two-beat rhythm. Without fine, effective aiding and well-developed impulsion coming from the horse, the transition will be awkward or even impossible.

The transitions between piaffe and passage are the next obstacle to overcome. The better prepared you are, the easier they will be. In working on the somewhat easier transition from the passage to the piaffe, the following factors are important: The horse should not be

"What I find fascinating about Klaus is his great empathy for horses and his feel for rhythm, a quality that's impossible to learn. I was able to learn a lot from him, especially when he rode my horses. Another great strength of his lies in his piaffe and passage work and his general calmness. As a rider Klaus demonstrates refined riding, and he also attaches great importance to his students riding with style and subtle aids."

MICHAEL KLIMKE
Grand Prix rider,
German champion

Bringing the horse back from the passage into the piaffe requires that the horse has a solid training foundation and is "through" to the aids.

In the transition into the passage the horse should lift himself forward-and-upward from an active hind leg into the prolonged phase of suspension.

worn out from riding round and round the arena in passage, rather, the rider should try to move the horse into the piaffe after only a few steps of passage. It is also important that the rider gives perfectly clear signals to the horse—that is, delivers his aids explicitly—which for the piaffe are a little different than for the passage. In the piaffe I apply the sensitive sustaining rein aids—they must never be "holding"—a little bit more strongly than in the passage. The forward driving leg aid, on the other hand, is used slightly less strongly. In both movements—piaffe and passage—it's important to not press with your legs but let them lie loosely on the horse's sides, giving only specific, brief directives. The better a horse reacts, the less intense these impulses have to be. In the course of his basic training, the horse should have learned how to develop impulsion from light leg aids.

If I now want to transition from passage into piaffe, I "play the horse back" a bit, that is, I put the horse in a head-and-neck position that's minimally deeper than usual, half-halt a little, and apply the aids for the piaffe, possibly supported by a tap with the whip. In this case, I prefer to apply the whip on top of the croup. This not only helps the horse lower his haunches, but also prevents using an aid that's directed toward only one hind leg, which could provoke uneven steps behind.

When I first try these transitions, I'm content with a few piaffe steps, and then I ride forward at the trot again. Gradually they will become more and more unconstrained and fluid—depending on the horse's talent, willingness to learn, and how well he's been prepared. Only then do I prolong the passage and piaffe phases, since only then has the horse developed the necessary strength to sustain them. The horse will also need this strength for the most difficult transition: the one from the piaffe into the passage. If the rider has succeeded in achieving a piaffe with hindquarters that are active and carrying, this transition is now possible—provided the rider allows himself and his horse time in the transition. If the rider transitions out of the piaffe suddenly, in an assault-like manner, the horse will most likely lose the rhythm. The less experienced the horse is, the more time he should be allowed to get from the piaffe into the passage. A mature, well-trained horse can of course complete this change more quickly.

The rider needs to take his time in the transition itself, as well the preparatory work leading up to it.

The transition from piaffe to passage is an important indicator of the quality of the piaffe. A good piaffe can be recognized by a seamless transition. For this reason, this is a very important transition.

In actuality, my piaffe and passage work consists mainly of improving the transitions. The transitions—early in training the "normal" ones between the different tempos and gaits, and later the ones between piaffe steps and passage-like steps—overlap. The better the transitions, the better the piaffe and passage will be, and vice versa.

CORRECTING PIAFFE-PASSAGE TRANSITIONS

Problems with piaffe-passage transitions are always a result of deficient preparation. These transitions are among the most difficult exercises there are because they're ultimately the result of years of work and are only successful when the horse is perfectly "through" and on the aids and correctly strengthened. The best way to eliminate difficulty is to return to the basics, consistently working on the components of the Training Scale again. Rhythm, suppleness and relaxation, contact, impulsion, straightness, and collection—when asked whether all of these qualities are existent in the horse, the rider must be able to answer with a confident "Yes!" before tackling the difficult transitions again. Depending on the horse's age and degree of deficiencies in his training, necessary corrections can take months, and sometimes even years.

WORK IN HAND

When schooling the piaffe and passage, opinions differ as to the pros and cons of in-hand work. Some people consider it absolutely necessary, while others reject it. My position is a bit in between. Work in hand requires a lot of feel. I don't generally work from the ground but prefer to teach the highly collected movements from the saddle because from there the rider must trigger the movements in the dressage arena. For some horses, however, support from the ground helps them to understand what's being asked of them. It can also serve to develop (or re-develop) impulsion. For me, the use of in-hand work depends on the individual horse.

The whip, however, I mainly apply on top of the croup, and only when riding. This way I prevent the horse from stepping unevenly behind.

When working from the ground, Klaus Balkenhol applies the whip mostly on the top of the croup.

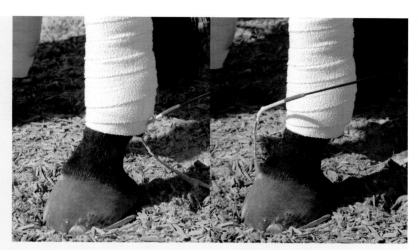

The different places to apply the whip when working in hand:

At the back of the fetlock (left).

At the front of the fetlock (right).

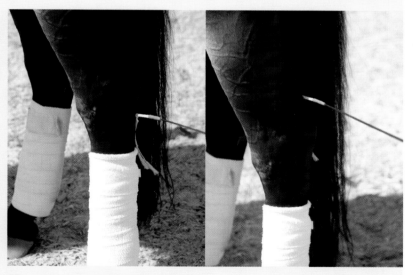

Below the hock (left).

Above the hock (right).

On the section of the croup where the tail originates (left).

On the front section of the croup (right).

DEVELOPING, IMPROVING, ELIMINATING FAULTS:
TEMPI CHANGES

The tempi changes, especially the one-tempi changes, are the next big challenge in a Grand Prix test. As usual, proper preparation in accordance with the Training Scale is absolutely necessary. The more secure the rhythm, the more supple the horse is, the more impulsion he has, and the straighter the counter-canter, then the better and more expressive the tempi changes will be.

Before I begin the one-tempi changes, I make sure that the preceding tempi changes (those at every second, or third stride, etc.) are solid. If the horse reacts to light aids and remains relaxed, I approach the one-tempi changes via the so-called "one-one" exercise. In other words, I let the horse make a single pair of changes: most horses find it easy to change from the true canter to the counter-canter and immediately back again to the true canter. If the horse understands and completes the one-one exercise without getting excited, I repeat it a

In the one-tempi changes (here Steffen Peters on Floriano), the horse should change the canter lead from stride to stride in a perfectly straight line ...

few canter strides later down the long side the arena, and depending on his reaction, I may repeat it four or five times.

As soon as this exercise goes so well that the canter rhythm remains even, I ask for three changes in a row, and again depending on how the horse reacts, perhaps even four or five changes. Some horses understand the exercise very quickly, while others require more time. Theoretically every horse is able to learn one-tempi changes, although their quality depends on the character of the horse's natural canter stride and also on his temperament. If the horse naturally has a good upward canter "jump" and is even-tempered, the one-tempi changes can—and should—be lofty and confident. However, fundamental gait problems can have a very negative influence on the tempi changes, and improvement in such cases is only possible to a certain degree.

The aids for the tempi changes should be as invisible as possible. If the rider uses his body too strongly, whether it's his legs, upper body, or hands, he will prevent success more than he furthers it.

"Klaus Balkenhol is a trainer who has an incredible amount of feel—for me one of the best there is. It is hard to find trainers anymore who are able to teach like him and also get on the horse themselves and demonstrate what they're teaching. That ability is unique!"

GUENTER SEIDEL
US Olympic medalist, dressage trainer

...while "jumping through" with both hind legs evenly forward and under him...

...and in the moment of changing ...

...there should be a clearly visible jump forward-and-upward, as seen here.

CORRECTING FAULTS IN THE ONE-TEMPI CHANGES

SIDEWAYS-SWINGING HINDQUARTERS: There are different reasons why some horses do this. They may not stride evenly toward both of the rider's hands, or the horse could be slightly ticklish and therefore sensitive to the rider's leg—a trait often seen in mares. Perhaps the rider laterally sways his body as he asks for the changes, which causes the horse to lose his balance.

In the first instance, I recommend working the horse increasingly "over his back" and directing the impulsion from the hindquarters forward. This can be achieved by riding transitions and working on bent lines. While in the flying changes themselves, the rider should ride more forward. It can also be helpful to practice tempi changes on large, bending lines.

When working with a ticklish horse, the rider must try to ride the changes with less lower leg and rely instead on a slight rotation of the hips. Riding more forward when in the changes also helps.

"Swaying" caused by a rider's incorrect seat can only be eliminated if the rider becomes aware of his problem. He should ride all lead changes—even a single change—either toward a mirror or while having someone videotape him. Recognizing his problem visually will help him eliminate it.

A HIGH CROUP: In this case, the rider should improve the horse's carrying power in the canter. On the one hand this is achieved, of course, by strengthening the entire horse, but it also necessitates special strengthening in the canter specifically. For this I intersperse work in normal collected canter with brief segments of extreme collection, both on straight and bent lines, especially in working canter pirouettes. This creates an uphill tendency, which I can then take into the tempi changes.

UNEVEN "JUMPING THROUGH": When the horse's training has been less than optimal, the horse may "jump through" the changes unevenly. In this case I would first go back to the basics, reviewing and reworking the individual elements of the Training Scale. As I would do for a horse that swayed sideways, I then ride the lead changes on a bent line in both directions. This gives me better control over the forward stride of each inner hind leg, respectively, while at the same time improving the contact.

WHAT MAKES RIDING ART?

If you ask Klaus Balkenhol what he feels constitutes the "art of riding," he doesn't have to think for long. "Riding is like painting. Many people are able to paint beautifully—for example, they may be able to create a lifelike horse. But only a few are able to go beyond this and also express the nature and soul of a horse and its movements. Riding is similar. There are many craftsmen and only a few artists."

In equestrian sport there are many craftsmen but only very few artists.

Having said that, Balkenhol doesn't want to devaluate the craftsmen among riders, but rather emphasizes that great success can also be achieved via pure technique. In his view, though, success cannot necessarily be reduced to simply winning medals in competitions.

"One can be successfully involved with horses on many different levels: from the saddle, from the ground, or from a driving vehicle, both recreationally and competitively," he explains. "For me, the 'art of riding' doesn't have so much to do with technique, which I simply rather take for granted. It implies more—much more. It can be learned only to a certain degree. The greater part has to do with giftedness, talent, and feel—the feel for understanding a horse and adapting to it. This you are born with."

Was Klaus Balkenhol born with this? His students from all over the world would doubtlessly agree without hesitation; he, however, simply shakes his head slowly, smiling, and emphasizes once more: "You cannot master the art of riding in one lifetime. The more you ride, the more you sense how much you still don't know, and how much you can learn from each new horse you ride."

The art of riding can only be learned to a certain extent—the other part one must be born with.

Those who know Balkenhol know too that this "Socratic attitude" *(All I know is that I know nothing)* is not void of meaning. Balkenhol really believes it. Instead of easily coasting on his knowledge, it instead serves as a daily incentive for him to learn more about each horse's nature, behavior, and individuality, and in this way gain even more "equestrian wisdom." The latter, he believes, lies in the ability to tune into each individual horse instead of merely making him obedient by applying a rigid training regimen. "Furthermore," Balkenhol claims, "the artist gains the ability to anticipate what his horse will do in the next moment and thus he can intuitively act and

An equestrian craftsman corrects mistakes, an equestrian artist intuitively feels mistakes and prevents them before they happen.

prevent a possible mistake. The rider who only reacts, on the other hand, will always remain a craftsman. A horse's natural grace will only truly manifest itself through the tuned-in artist, and even the layman spectator will be able to sense the harmony between horse and rider."

This doesn't mean that Balkenhol's training method consists of spoiling and pampering his horses. Skill as a rider, including consistent aids, is just as important to him—and he conscientiously serves as a living example for his students every day. An energetic aid with the leg or spur instead of constant banging; a purposeful touch with the whip at the right moment—always followed by praise when the horse responds in the desired manner—maintains (or makes) his horses sensitive and furthers their desire to perform and enjoy their work.

"Consistency must rule from the very beginning so that the horse learns what the human expects from him," says Balkenhol. "The rider must never break or dominate the horse's will, though—he must only show the way. For instance, with Goldstern I had to be quite firm because he had, despite his nervousness, a very strong character. He needed human leadership in order to be able to fully develop his potential and find harmony with a rider."

At Balkenhol's stable, this "firmness" is always applied with the horse's well-being in mind: consistency is used instead of pressure, and trainers are sympathetic instead of attempting to dominate the horse. The horses are grateful for this treatment, which is demonstrated by their competitive successes. In the course of his 30-year career, Balkenhol has brought about 20 horses to the Grand Prix level or to international acclaim.

Although he's been a competitive rider half his life, Balkenhol isn't ignorant of the dangers of catering to this kind of athletic focal point. "Especially when riding dressage tests—that is, asking for certain movements specifically at predetermined spots in the arena—the artistic approach (which should be the true nature of dressage) can incidentally fall by the wayside," he says.

Especially when riding dressage tests in competition, one is often in danger of losing sight of the "artistic aspect" of equestrian sport.

Anyone who regularly rides tests knows what Balkenhol means. Dressage's required movements must be performed in certain spots in the arena, regardless whether the horse is optimally set up for the movement at a particular moment or not. "If need be, experienced riders know how to 'cheat' through a movement without most of the audience noticing," Balkenhol admits. "But when that is the case the magic of true artistic interplay between horse and rider, the moment of perfect harmony from which a movement is created, will fail to appear."

Klaus Balkenhol focuses on harmony between horse and rider.

Is this Balkenhol's rejection of competitive riding? "No," the Olympic medalist says, laughing. "Although it's true I've become calmer and more patient now that I don't show anymore myself, I wouldn't only want to work with horses and riders in solitude and privacy, like in a museum. For me, competitive sport is an integral element of riding. However, I do believe that one mustn't sacrifice art for competitive success. Every rider should always ask himself in everything he pursues on horseback if it's still about harmony with the horse, which should be the absolute core of all riding, or is it actually about creating effects, spectacular show, or even business and monetary gain."

I wouldn't want to ride and train horses as if we were in a museum, simply preserved and never tested.

Harmony with the horse is what Balkenhol feels characterizes a good rider and is what he expects from every rider. He also emphasizes the ability to have sympathy for the horse—when problems arise, the rider should always look at himself first for the possible cause.

Balkenhol expects the following from every rider:

- **Flexibility and consistency**
- **Sympathy and feel**
- **Patience**
- **Clarity of aids and communication with the horse**
- **Diligence (without false ambition)**
- **Horsemanship**

Balkenhol deliberately uses the expression "every rider." For him, "true artists, meaning those who have talent, skill, and feel for the horse are rare, even at the highest levels," he says. "But I believe that through horsemanship, diligence, and practice everyone can achieve certain skills that enable him to celebrate his riding—even without showing. To me, someone who rides in harmony with his horse at Second Level in his backyard is closer to being an 'artist' than someone who competes at Third or Fourth Level through coarseness and forceful influence."

KLAUS BALKENHOL'S
GREATEST ACHIEVEMENTS AS A RIDER

1979 German reserve champion with Rabauke

1988 European champion of the police riders

1990 German reserve champion with Goldstern

1991 Team European champion and European reserve champion in the Freestyle (individual) with Goldstern; German champion with Goldstern

1992 Team Olympic gold medalist and individual Olympic bronze medalist in Barcelona with Goldstern; German champion with Goldstern

1993 Team European champion with Goldstern; German champion with Goldstern

1994 Team World Cup champion and reserve World Cup champion individual/Freestyle with Goldstern

1995 German champion with Goldstern; team European champion and sixth place individually

1996 Team Olympic gold medalist and sixth place individually with Goldstern; German champion with Goldstern

Furthermore, in the years between 1993 and 1996 alone, Balkenhol won or placed in more than 90 national and international Grand Prix, Grand Prix Special, and Grand Prix Freestyle classes with the horses Goldstern, Ehrengold, Laudatio, Gracioso, Nikolaus, and Garçon. Before that he had success with Rabauke, Mon Petit, Askat, Acapulco, Aponti, Sylvester, Escorial, and Rhodomo.

THE RIGHT COACHING

The rider who only gets to sit on a horse like a "wooden board" will never achieve the correct feeling for seat and aiding.

This harmonious interplay between horse and rider is the result of years of hard work, especially on oneself. This is because good dressage riding (which has hopefully become "art" at some point!) has a lot to do with the ability to concentrate on hundreds of little things simultaneously, without looking strained. This cannot be learned overnight—and it cannot be learned alone.

"This requires a riding instructor," Balkenhol emphasizes. "The instructor must manage to teach his student the right techniques without mentally overwhelming him. This is only possible on a well-trained horse. How else can the student learn to feel the difference between right and wrong? Only when he knows how a smooth half-halt feels, for example, can he learn to apply the aids correctly, memorize them, and then begin to use them unconsciously—without forgetting everything else he has to do—when performing. A rider at a lower to medium performance level sometimes isn't able to feel his horse's balance and impulsion. How can he ever learn to do this on a young or badly trained horse? An instructor can only teach a student what it feels like when a horse 'swings,' is on the aids, and is supple with a horse that's been trained accordingly. The student who only has the opportunity to sit on a 'wooden board'—pardon my expression—will never get the right feel for seat and aiding but instead will only grow accustomed to pulling, yanking, and being yanked on.

"Only a rider who has learned how it feels when the horse is moving correctly can develop, correctly internalize, and automate the ability to recreate such movement. And, this is also the only way it's possible to think about—or better: to feel—all the numerous little things that are important in riding and eventually come to a point where you can ride autonomously."

Balkenhol wants to not only teach his students how to become autonomous riders, he also wants to preserve and further their abilities. Admittedly, Balkenhol doesn't have any beginner students at this time. The days of explaining how to mount a horse to his young colleagues in the police squadron are past. Today, Balkenhol has students from all over the world, many of them top international riders

"Klaus Balkenhol is one of the best coaches and riders I have ever known. All of his horses are extremely supple and go very loosely 'over the back'—therefore, they are all also particularly good at piaffe and passage. As a coach, Klaus always has the overall view in mind. He not only works on individual movements and lessons, but also tries to always recognize and improve the general context of the lesson, and its causes and effects. He is very calm, never demonstrating sudden anger, which is an extremely important trait in the discipline of dressage."

HUBERTUS SCHMIDT
Dressage trainer, Olympic team medalist, team World champion, German master rider and trainer

Since Klaus Balkenhol has ridden horses of all types and temperaments in all movements, he is good at explaining to his students from the ground how to do things, and also what it should feel like.

as well as promising young talents who generally have already reached at least Fourth Level before working with him. But despite his immense success, Balkenhol has remained true to his roots in matters of horse training. "I started from nothing but had the opportunity to learn a lot every day I worked with horses. For the sake of all horses and their future riders, I want to pass along my knowledge to as many riders as possible—not only the top riders."

Balkenhol juggles his desire to teach with the little free time he has by holding and attending seminars and clinics. They are always very successful and questions from the participants are usually intelligent and multifaceted. "I'm always pleased by how interested people are in learning about the classical way of training horses," says Balkenhol.

Only by riding a well-trained horse, will a rider learn how to "feel."

What he "preaches" at these events—how to train a horse according to the principles of the Training Scale and with sympathy for the horse and its needs—he also communicates when teaching his students. He relies, despite all his coaching from the ground, on his riders' independence. "I distinguish a little bit between an 'instructor' and a 'trainer,' which I think of as a 'coach,'" he explains. "A riding instructor's goal is to teach someone technical skills. A trainer's goal goes beyond that. He must also not only be able to teach, he must be able to optimize his students'—and their horses'—skills."

Few others know how to do this like Balkenhol. Just as he was able (and is still) to sensitively "tune in" to all the different horses he rode during his career as a competitor, so does he deal with"his" riders.

Klaus Balkenhol relies on his riders' independence—besides all the help he offers from the ground.

"As a coach, one must never try to fundamentally alter a student's individual riding characteristics," he emphasizes. "Instead, one must guide him in the right direction—but in a way the rider isn't aware of." Why is this? "Otherwise I'd deprive the rider of his self-confidence and also his autonomy—two qualities without which he would never ever achieve success again," Balkenhol says.

So, instead of telling his students something along the lines of, "What you're doing is totally wrong—do it this way or that way," the experienced trainer uses his vast knowledge to subtly convince his students to follow his lead and allow him to guide them in the right direction. For example, if a rider is doing a flying change and the horse continually evades sideways, Balkenhol will say: "Why don't you flex him a little less in the new direction—or even briefly counter-flex him?" The change will turn out straight, and the rider will notice the difference and so adjust his way of aiding in the future.

It's this eye for detail that enthuses Balkenhol's students so much, in addition to the fact that he is able to demonstrate everything he teaches on horseback himself. If his verbal explanation isn't enough, he mounts without hesitating, rides a few rounds, feels what's going on, solves the problem, and then knows better what advice to give the rider. "I believe that a trainer should be able to demonstrate everything he teaches so that the student can see just from watching what needs to change," he says. "Sadly, however, today there are far too many 'trainers' who have no true understanding of dressage and, above all, are not proficient in it."

There's no doubt Balkenhol knows about dressage. Not only did he earn Olympic medals during his own riding career, he also trained Nadine Capellmann, a two-time World Cup winner, for many years, and he coached his daughter, Anabel, to successes at Grand Prix level, as well as young rider, Carola Koppelmann, and the Danish Olympic rider, Princess Nathalie zu Sayn-Wittgenstein. Balkenhol also led—after taking a detour to train the German dressage team—the US dressage team to the top of international competition.

What else constitutes a good coach and trainer—apart from the ability to demonstrate everything he teaches on horseback? Many instructors may in fact be able to do this, but only a few have the skill to combine it with giving lessons that are good as well as motivating.

> "What I particularly like—apart from the vast amount of knowledge that Klaus Balkenhol is able to instill in his students, of course—is that he allows his students their freedom and makes them feel secure. This kind of coaching on a psychological level I find just as important as the technical component."
>
> **STEFFEN PETERS**
> US Olympic team rider, dressage trainer

An instructor should be able to demonstrate what he teaches.

BALKENHOL'S RECIPE FOR GOOD COACHING

A good coach:

▶ must first and foremost recognize and accept each rider's individuality.

▶ should be familiar with what the rider is probably feeling on the horse and be able to instruct him accordingly.

▶ doesn't simply say things like, "more hindquarters"—he must give advice on the "how" and "what" so that the rider can practically translate it into his riding.

▶ doesn't yell but also doesn't let the rider get away with mistakes. He takes steps to influence the rider before the mistake happens. For example, this can be achieved by having a

A few tips from the side of the ring make Tip Top, ridden by Leslie Morse, move more beautifully with better contact.

student repeatedly practice a difficult movement and analyzing the situation. The coach must help the rider understand what it is he's doing up there (on the horse's back) and why what he is doing does or doesn't work.

► might have to punish—not the horse but the rider who lacks concentration. If necessary the rider must dismount and quit for the day. Then he has enough time to think about his mistakes.

► continually directs his student's attention to the solving of a problem until the rider does it unconsciously, thereby creating the necessary prerequisites to eliminate it completely.

► encourages his student instead of discouraging him. He should frustrate neither the student nor the horse by asking too much of them, nor bore them by under-challenging them.

▸ is able to convey the correct feeling to the student because he knows how it feels himself.

▸ knows that failure in producing the correct movement must never lead to frustration.

▸ doesn't make his student dependent on him, but teaches him to become independent as a rider.

Highly concentrated and always focused: Coach Klaus Balkenhol, teaching.

The last item on the list is of particular importance to Balkenhol. Too often he has seen riders completely fail in the show ring when their instructor isn't standing by their side. "This must never be allowed to happen," he explains. "A rider who rides well and correctly at his level at home can also do so in the show ring—without the presence of his trainer. If, however, the trainer has given the rider the feeling that nothing works without him, he has created a state of mental dependency in the rider. The student's self-confidence has

My riders must also be able to cope by themselves.

THINK QUICKLY

The rider who acts out of frustration, attempting to improve faulty performance with harsh measures and countless repetitions, chooses the wrong path. Infinite repetitions of one and the same problematic movement are usually a sign of insecurity in the rider and serve no purpose other than self-satisfaction. The horse doesn't gain anything from it. It leads to an overwrought horse and causes muscle fatigue and nervousness. Here, a trainer must intervene and go back to easier exercises rider and horse have already mastered.

The rider must learn to think quickly and anticipate the moment where a mistake commonly occurs. For example: if a rider has difficulty with the pirouette, he cannot solve the larger problem by practicing the pirouette over and over again. Instead, the rider should focus on controlling every single canter stride within the pirouette. That's what he must work on systematically and patiently—not the pirouette itself.

now been weakened, which has a negative effect on his riding. To make matters worse, if the rider attempts to ride without his trainer's aid and is unsuccessful, then he is confirmed in his belief that he absolutely needs the presence of his trainer. That's fatal."

This doesn't mean, of course, that Balkenhol leaves his riders alone at shows. Whenever possible, he accompanies them to the big shows, coaches them during their preparation, and gives advice in the warm-up. "I'm not able to be everywhere, of course," he admits, "and therefore my riders need to be able to cope on their own. I want them to not only follow my instructions, but also be able to understand them and put them into the big picture. Only this way will they progress in their daily training, and only this way will their horses really benefit."

"What I particularly like about Klaus is that he's so calm and patient. Never ever do his lessons become frenzied; he completely tunes into his students. I also find it amazing that he mounts his students' horses and feels and demonstrates from the saddle. I'm able to relate to many things and understand things better by watching and witnessing how the horse develops. This tells me what I need to work on. Klaus also builds his students up, always giving them confidence, suggesting that 'you'll be able to get this as well.' Training with him has always helped me a lot."

INGRID KLIMKE
Eventer, Olympian, team World Cup champion, multiple German champion, successful Grand Prix rider, dressage and event trainer

When Klaus Balkenhol explains something, even the horses seem to listen.

A rider should not only follow instructions but must also see the big picture.

When preparing for a show, as well as when at the show itself, experience is required, both in rider and coach. The less experienced the rider, the more the coach has to instruct him—this is true for both daily workouts and preparation in the warm-up arena. Balkenhol sometimes deals with riders who have little experience, perhaps not as riders, but as competitors at the Grand Prix level. Introducing such riders to the highest level in the sport of dressage is a particular interest of his. For this reason, he supported a special series of tests addressed to those who wish to take the plunge from the Young Riders level to the Grand Prix level. "Here the coaching is of particular significance," Balkenhol says. "As a trainer, one not only has to improve and refine the student's technical skills but also the mental development of the athlete."

He focuses particularly on coaching for competitions, that is, the technical monitoring of the rider from preparation at home to entering the show ring, and lists the following trainer guidelines as all-important:

▸ The coach must guide both rider and horse to a level of reciprocal communication.

▸ The coach must instill confidence in the rider to prevent anxiety,

US rider Guenter Seidel and Klaus Balkenhol working with Aragon shortly before the CHIO Aachen.

nervousness, and insecurity. This is only possible through optimal preparation and a reasonable amount of mentoring at competitions.

▶ Preparation at home should include a simulated show and test situation. This is the only way a rider will learn to assess himself, the horse, and the horse's possible reactions.

▸ Without participating in shows, there is no show experience. Therefore—provided that the rider copes with test requirements at home without any problems—the coach should encourage the student to compete instead of sitting at home, dreaming of it because of a fear of failure.

▸ The coach should choose the "right" shows and discuss them with the rider, that is, such shows where the competition is neither too big (risking the rider getting frustrated) nor too little (risking the rider overestimating his capabilities in the future).

▸ The coach must know the rider and horse so well so that he can tune into each individually. This requires a great amount of experience both as a rider and a teacher.

▸ During competition, the coach should work to encourage the rider instead of frustrating him. This includes having him start out with simple movements in the warm-up, which the rider will be able to execute successfully, thereby giving him security and preventing him from getting nervous.

▸ Movements that the rider and horse struggle with should be practiced sparingly in the warm-up. The rider won't be able to improve them in the few minutes before a test, but they'll easily sap the rider's confidence and the harmony between rider and horse.

▸ The coach should teach his student to ride in the warm-up arena in the same way as he would ride at home. This means calmly loosening up the horse, then building from easy exercises to more difficult ones and not allowing external influences to become unsettling.

▸ During the warm-up, the coach should only give tips instead of critiquing. The latter causes the rider to become insecure or tense—both of which are poor prerequisites for a successful ride.

KLAUS BALKENHOL'S
GREATEST ACHIEVEMENTS AS A TRAINER

1996 Student Nadine Capellmann is reserve rider for the German team in the Olympic Games, Atlanta, Georgia, United States

1997 Coaches German team to gold medal at European Championships, with the individual gold medal (Isabell Werth), individual bronze medal (Karin Rehbein), and fourth-place individual score (Nadine Capellmann) in Verden, Germany

1998 Coaches German team to gold medal at the World Cup, with the individual gold medal (Isabell Werth), and fourth-place individual score (Karin Rehbein) in Rome, Italy

1999 Coaches German team to gold medal at the European Championships, with the individual silver medal (Ulla Salzgeber) in Arnheim, The Netherlands

2000 Coaches German team to Olympic gold medal, with the individual silver medal (Isabell Werth), and individual bronze medal (Ulla Salzgeber) in Sydney, Australia

2002 Nadine Capellmann wins double World Cup gold medals (team and individual) and coaches US team to silver medal in Jerez, Spain

2004 Coaches US team to Olympic bronze medal, with fourth-place individual score (Debbie McDonald) in Athens, Greece

2006 Coaches US team to World Cup bronze medal, with fourth-place individual score (Steffen Peters) in Aachen, Germany

Furthermore, in 2002 and 2003 he was elected "Trainer of the Year" in the US. Balkenhol has been Nadine Capellmann's trainer for 13 years, and has trained many other successful riders such as Hubertus Schmidt, Nathalie zu Sayn-Wittgenstein, Anabel Balkenhol, Carola Koppelmann, Ingrid and Michael Klimke, Bettina Hoy, and Helen Langehanenberg.

MAINTAINING ENJOYMENT

Too much ambition causes more harm than good.

"Laugh! Riding is supposed to be fun." This light-hearted, silly sentence is often tossed at riders who are concentrating and therefore have a scowling look on their face. There is a grain of truth in it, though. Of course, one does need to concentrate when riding. However, riding is supposed to be enjoyable, regardless whether it is a leisurely trail ride or striving for the highest levels in dressage. Many a rider's face might raise doubts about this when he's seen pursuing his "hobby," his passion, so grimly.

"It's a question of ambition," Balkenhol believes. And Klaus Balkenhol, the trainer, knows that "when there's too much of it, it causes more harm than good." In his time as an active competitive rider he had to deal with his own ambition and impatience. He learned to keep his ambition and yet curb it. "I believe I've done quite a good job with it," he says with a smile, reminiscing. "But it's not easy, especially if there are important shows coming up. Then a rider's tendency is to simply put more pressure on himself and his horse—unfortunately, this is sometimes more than is good for either of them. More often than not, pressure doesn't make things better— it makes them worse. With all the ambition a rider might have, he must maintain a certain amount of serenity or he will lose the joy of riding along the way."

One can tell that Balkenhol, now over 65 years old, has maintained this "joy" to this day. His seat, position, and facial expression while on the horse's back suggest deep satisfaction. When something goes wrong, Balkenhol remains calm, and simply gives the movement another try. When everything works to his satisfaction, his face just beams with pleasure as he enthusiastically explains what he has done differently, where the mistake lay, and why this horse in particular was able to respond correctly only now.

There are no signs of "burn out" in Balkenhol. "Riding is still something very special in my life," he says. "Nonetheless, creating knock-your-socks-off, brilliant performances are not necessarily my priority. Instead my focus is that I as a human being make the horse understand me, and that I learn to understand the horse and am al-

> "What makes Klaus Balkenhol stand out as a trainer for me is his great feel, and his sympathy for the horses. Also his ability to make a horse feel good about everything it is supposed to learn and enjoy it, instead of stressing the horse out. Klaus seems to know exactly how far he can go without ever running the risk of asking too much of a horse. And I think that he is a very sincere, very authentic person, which also characterizes the style of his training."

DEBBIE MCDONALD
US team rider, Olympian, World Cup gold medalist, dressage trainer, multiple-time US "Rider of the Year"

lowed to contribute my part to keeping him happy. This mutual communication—that's where the fascination of riding lies for me."

Speaking of happy horses: all the horses living at Balkenhol's
facility seem to be content—the youngsters as well as the retirees,
the competition horses as well as the farm's senior pony, Muskatnuss ("Nutmeg" in English). It's very important to the entire
Balkenhol family that the facility's four-legged inhabitants feel
good and are happy.

*For me the real
fascination lies in
mutual communication
between rider and horse.*

Dealing with horses and
training them carefully fills
Klaus Balkenhol with joy, even
after more than 50 years of
riding and training.

When a horse moves the way Klaus Balkenhol expects him to, you can often see a smile sneak along his lips.

"The use of the phrase 'happy horse' that has gained popularity lately in competitive circles is a legitimate postulation, which should, in fact, be a matter of course," says Balkenhol. "But when I look at the facial expressions and body languages of many competitive mounts, I have doubts as to whether these horses are really 'happy.' A horse that constantly swishes his tail, puts his ears back, has agitated eyes, is full of tension, is on edge and won't remain standing in a relaxed manner under his rider can't be very happy in my view. In some ways, I believe that the current use of the expression 'happy horse' is nothing more than a nice and catchy P.R. term."

Could it be that ultimately a horse's happiness can be found only in his rider "hitting the ground," as an old German proverb suggests? Balkenhol laughs. "No, of course not," he says. "If this was true, horses probably would have become nearly extinct by now and could only be seen in a zoo. But a horse's happiness does depend on many factors: on the way he's stabled and managed, which should be in accordance with his needs as much as possible; on the variety of activities he's offered, presenting a change from daily monotony; and on the way people deal with the horse in terms of ethical principles—both when riding and handling him. If all this is to the horse's satisfaction, a horse can be happy indeed."

Anyone who purchases a horse must be aware that he has bought a living creature.

Balkenhol is also very concerned about the responsibility every horse owner has for his horse. In his view, this responsibility is not tied to using the horse as a sport horse or to the horse's age. "The person who purchases a horse," he emphasizes, "regardless of what purpose the horse will serve, must be aware of the fact that he has bought a living creature, not a piece of sport or fun equipment. And, no matter how much one loves to ride, one's ambition must never become first priority in a relationship with a horse. Not all horses are born to become dressage athletes, for example, and only a few are born capable of competing at the top of the sport. A rider must realize this and always only demand from the horse what he can realistically give—even if this is a level lower than hoped for.

Riding and dealing with horses always has a character-building component.

"Riders and trainers must also never forget that a horse is a creature that makes mistakes in his work, just like a person does. These mistakes are not an intentional attempt to tease or torment the rider; they happen because there is a communication problem or because the horse is overtaxed by what the rider has asked, meaning that the rider himself has provoked the mistake. To punish a horse in such moments or take out anger that may have accumulated throughout the day on him, is irresponsible. For this reason, riding and dealing with horses always has a character-building component for people. I, the human being, have to tune into the horse, study him and learn as much about his nature, behavior, and needs as possible. A rider owes this to his horse. And, he can't simply get rid of the horse after he has no longer any use for him, say, once the horse retires from competition or the daily riding regimen. The responsibility that a horse owner has for his animals cannot be simply switched off or pushed away. It's a responsibility that lasts a lifetime. Old horses have a right to spend their sunset years joyfully. Throughout the years, our older animals have shown us again and again that horses can be happy and can also make people happy if they're kept and looked after accordingly. This is because a horse always remains a horse—with or without a rider."

Allowed to become a happy "oldie": 30-year-old Rabauke in his pasture at Balkenhol's farm in Germany.

ETHICAL PRINCIPLES FOR THE TRUE HORSEMAN[*]:

1 Anyone involved with a horse assumes responsibility for the creature entrusted to him.

2 The horse must be kept in a way that meets his natural living requirements

3 A horse's physical and mental well-being must be one's first priority regardless of its use.

4 Man must respect every horse alike, regardless of its breed, age, and sex, and its use for breeding, recreation, or competition.

5 Knowledge of the history of the horse, his needs, and how to handle him is part of our historic-cultural heritage. This information must be preserved, explained, and passed on to future generations.

6 Being around horses is a character-building experience and of valuable significance to the development of the human being—especially young people. This aspect must always be respected and promoted.

7 The human being who participates in equestrian sport with his horse must undergo training, and must also provide training for the horse entrusted to him. The goal of any training is to bring about the best possible harmony between human being and horse.

8 The use of the horse in competition as well as in general riding, driving, and vaulting must be geared toward the horse's ability, temperament, and willingness to perform. Manipulating a horse's capacity to perform by means of medication or other "horse-unfriendly" influences is to be rejected by all and people engaged in such practices should be prosecuted.

9 The responsibility a human has for the horse entrusted to him extends to the end of the horse's life. The human must always assume this responsibility and implement any decisions with the horse's well-being in mind.

*Source: German National Equestrian Federation (FN)

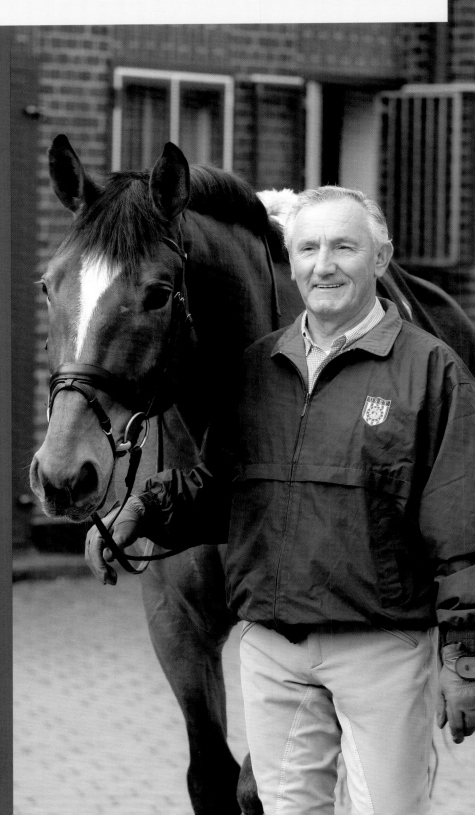

Also from Trafalgar Square:

Classical Schooling with the Horse in Mind
Gentle Gymnastic Training Techniques
Anja Beran
192 pp, 85 color and 25 b/w photos, 33 illustrations

Riding Logic
Transform Riding Skills to "Art on Horseback" with
Classical Lessons in Flatwork and Jumping
Wilhelm Müseler
176 pp, 58 color photos, 44 illustrations

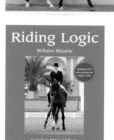

Tug of War: Classical versus "Modern" Dressage
Why Classical Schooling Works and How Incorrect,
"Modern" Training Negatively Affects Horses' Health
Dr. Gerd Heuschmann
144 pp, 76 color photos, 20 illustrations

Straightening the Crooked Horse
Correct Imbalance, Relieve Strain, and Encourage Free Movement
with an Innovative System of Straightness Training
Gabriele Rachen-Schöneich & Klaus Schöneich
160 pp, 50 color photos, 60 illustrations

The Ultimate Horse Behavior and Training Book
Enlightened and Revolutionary Solutions for the 21st Century
Linda Tellington-Jones with Bobbie Lieberman
344 pp, 364 color photos, 81 illustrations